# THE
# CONTAGIOUS
# POWER OF
# THINKING

# THE CONTAGIOUS POWER OF THINKING

## HOW YOUR THOUGHTS CAN INFLUENCE THE WORLD

## DAVID R. HAMILTON, PhD

HAY HOUSE

Australia • Canada • Hong Kong • India
South Africa • United Kingdom • United States

**First published and distributed in the United Kingdom by:**
Hay House UK Ltd, 292B Kensal Rd, London W10 5BE.
Tel.: (44) 20 8962 1230; Fax: (44) 20 8962 1239. www.hayhouse.co.uk

**Published and distributed in the United States of America by:**
Hay House, Inc., PO Box 5100, Carlsbad, CA 92018-5100. Tel.: (1) 760 431
7695 or (800) 654 5126; Fax: (1) 760 431 6948 or (800) 650 5115.
www.hayhouse.com

**Published and distributed in Australia by:**
Hay House Australia Ltd, 18/36 Ralph St, Alexandria NSW 2015.
Tel.: (61) 2 9669 4299; Fax: (61) 2 9669 4144. www.hayhouse.com.au

**Published and distributed in the Republic of South Africa by:**
Hay House SA (Pty), Ltd, PO Box 990, Witkoppen 2068.
Tel./Fax: (27) 11 467 8904. www.hayhouse.co.za

**Published and distributed in India by:**
Hay House Publishers India, Muskaan Complex, Plot No.3, B-2, Vasant Kunj,
New Delhi – 110 070. Tel.: (91) 11 4176 1620; Fax: (91) 11 4176 1630.
www.hayhouse.co.in

**Distributed in Canada by:**
Raincoast, 9050 Shaughnessy St, Vancouver, BC V6P 6E5.
Tel.: (1) 604 323 7100; Fax: (1) 604 323 2600

© David Hamilton, 2011

The moral rights of the author have been asserted.

The author of this book does not dispense medical advice or prescribe the use of any technique as a form of treatment for physical or medical problems without the advice of a physician, either directly or indirectly. The intent of the author is only to offer information of a general nature to help you in your quest for emotional and spiritual well-being. In the event you use any of the information in this book for yourself, which is your constitutional right, the author and the publisher assume no responsibility for your actions.

A catalogue record for this book is available from the British Library.

ISBN 978-1-84850-293-2

Printed and bound in Great Britain by
TJ International, Padstow, Cornwall.

**'*Ubuntu* is very difficult to render into a Western language… It is to say, "My humanity is caught up, is inextricably bound up, in what is yours."'**

Archbishop Desmond Tutu

# CONTENTS

# ACKNOWLEDGEMENTS

I am deeply grateful to my partner, Elizabeth Caproni, for her great patience when she hardly saw me during the last two months of writing this book and also for doing the first edit on every chapter and suggesting valuable content enhancements.

I am also grateful to my friend Bryce Redford for emailing me new studies he stumbled across that were useful in my research.

And I would like to say thank you to my editor, Lizzie Hutchins, for doing some 'literary sanding', smoothing the rough edges of my writing and making it a little easier on the reader's eye.

Thank you also to the staff at Hay House for supporting my development as a writer and teacher and for giving me the opportunity to reach so many people with this book and the ones that came before it.

And I'd like to say thank you to the staff of Starbucks in Windsor, the place I call my 'office', who supplied me with many cups of coffee and a nice atmosphere to write in.

# INTRODUCTION

I started writing this book because I wanted to show that kindness was contagious. One kind act, I had found when writing my last book, can inspire another person to perform a kind act, which in turn can inspire another, and so on.

Even though it might sound idealistic, I honestly believe that kindness can make the world a better place. Just as a lily pad in a pond will rise and fall on the wave produced by a pebble dropped in that pond, so acts of kindness will raise the spirits of people we might never know.

I soon realized that this effect isn't limited to acts of kindness. When you're happy, you make others happy. This isn't just because of what you say or because you might be acting a little more exuberantly, it's because they sense how you feel and it makes them feel the same way. Happiness is contagious.

There's nothing spooky about it. We all have cells in the brain called mirror neurons. They cause us to subtly copy the expressions of those around us. If a person is smiling, we smile. If a person is frowning, we frown. And our facial expressions inform our emotional state and so we begin to feel the same emotions as the people we spend time with. We are usually completely unaware that it's happening, but the longer we're around someone who is happy, the more their happiness will rub off on us.

Sadness and depression flow in the same way. Hanging around someone who is depressed is one sure-fire way to become more depressed yourself. Research at Harvard has even quantified it. If a friend of yours has become depressed for any reason, it increases the likelihood that you will also become depressed by 93 per cent.[1]

You might wonder how they figured this out. They used data from a social network of over 12,000 people and tracked how their mental health changed in response to the mental health changes of their social contacts. It turns out that the chance of catching depression from another person actually depends upon our relationship with them. The stronger the friendship, the greater the contagiousness.

It works the same with happiness.[2] A happy friend can increase the probability of you becoming happy by 25 per cent, but a happy best friend can increase your likelihood by 63 per cent, because you're emotionally closer. Bring on the happy friends!

It turns out that the more friends and social contacts you have, the greater your likelihood of happiness and the lower your likelihood of depression. And because we live in such a socially interconnected world, our emotions don't just affect the people we're friends or even acquaintances with. We transmit our mood to our friends' friends' friends, and they to us.

Emotions also transmit to children and even babies. A mother can pick up on her infant's feelings and the infant can also feel the mother's. This is all well and good if a child grows up in a happy household, but if the parents are always fighting then the child will absorb their toxic emotions like a sponge and this will affect its development.

There can be escape in such households to the world of video games, but only if they're non-violent games. Reams of research now shows that children who play violent video games become more aggressive and show less empathy than children who don't play them.

Just about anything you think, say and do is contagious. Habits, for example, are contagious. That's good if they're healthy habits, but obviously not if they are unhealthy ones. Obesity, for instance, is quite contagious and, just like depression and happiness, we can be infected by our friends' friends' friends. Literally, your sister's hairdresser's best friend can make you fat. At least there's a 10 per cent chance of it, according to research.[3]

Through the contagiousness of unhealthy habits, even non-contagious medical conditions can become contagious. Heart disease, for instance, can spread from person to person. It isn't contagious in that it spreads through the transmission of bacteria or a virus; it spreads from mind to mind. All we need to do is copy the unhealthy diet and lifestyle of someone who is preparing for an early grave and we increase the risk that we will follow them.

Fear is also contagious. It can result in mass hysteria, which is actually much more common than you might think. It shows itself on a fairly regular basis, disguised as outbreaks of chemical or food poisoning, when there are no chemicals or bad food, only fear, which spreads from person to person until it infects a whole town.

The workplace provides a fertile ground for the contagion of emotions. Many studies show that the success of teams is heavily influenced by the mood of one or two individuals. If a leader is happy, it can lift the mood of the team, and if they are sad or angry, it can lower the mood.

In fact the moods of leaders are so contagious that they actually affect the bottom line. A study of a large retail chain showed that for each one-point increase in a manager's job satisfaction, there was a 5 per cent increase in customer spending.[4]

The mood in all teams affects performance. A study of penalty shootouts from 151 World Cup and European Championship football matches even found that the players who celebrated more positively after scoring their penalties were more likely to be on the winning side.[5]

Can we use this knowledge to make a difference to the world around us? Yes! You only need to flash a smile at someone to raise a smile in them. No matter how hard they may try to resist, smiling is contagious. And according to the 'facial feedback hypothesis', which postulates that facial movement can affect emotional experience, smiling can actually make us feel happier.

So we can spread happiness just by smiling at people, and of course smiling at yourself in the mirror helps too – regardless of how embarrassing that might seem!

There are no isolated acts. We live in an interconnected world where emotions, attitudes and behaviour travel from person to person to person, infecting everyone they touch. And such is the wiring in our brains that we literally sense some of the world through others. In a very real way, other people are extensions of ourselves. We share part of their experience of the world. It's unavoidable.

It's called emotional contagion.

# 'I FEEL IT FROM YOUR FACE'

### 'Alas, after a certain age every man is responsible for his face.'
Albert Camus

John enters a room full of people talking amongst themselves. Sarah is chatting to Rebecca. She is annoyed because her boss hasn't noticed the good job she's been doing and has continually passed her up for promotion. She worries that she isn't showing as much confidence as her colleagues, even though she is doing a better job.

John is sporting a large smile. He is upright, his shoulders are back and he is walking with an air of grace, inner contentment and confidence. A few people notice him as he enters the room. Sarah is one of them. She sees his smile and immediately finds herself smiling in his direction and losing her train of thought in speaking to Rebecca. She shakes her head and then tells Rebecca about the previous weekend, when she went on a date with Mike.

Within five minutes John is enjoying a conversation with a small group. They all seem to be relaxed. Everyone is smiling and there are a few little bursts of laughter. Andrea, Jo and Ian had been expressing their disapproval of the new government education policy earlier, but now their conversation has shifted to talking about their forthcoming holidays.

In a nearby group, the conversation has also shifted and people seem much less tense than before.

These shifts are not unrelated. In fact John's mood is contagious. It is spreading through the room like the aroma of a scented candle.

Moods spread from brain to brain – not via a virus or any mysterious route, but due to the action of interconnected groups of cells in the brain called mirror neurons. These neurons enable us to unconsciously read the facial expressions of other people and mirror them. They also read the physical body movements of others and mirror those too, effectively reproducing the body language of others. In fact this is how they were first discovered. Scientists noticed that when macaque monkeys watched the grasping movements of other monkeys, the same regions of their brains were activated as when they made the moves themselves.[1]

Up until 2010, most of the evidence for the existence of mirror neurons in humans had been inferred from brain-imaging studies. Then scientists at UCLA jumped at the chance to study the brains of patients with intractable epilepsy during clinical investigations which offered the unique opportunity to study single cells in the brain.[2]

Electrodes were implanted in 21 patients to try to identify the locations of the seizures. The scientists then asked the patients to watch videos of people performing hand gestures and making facial expressions and then perform them themselves. They recorded activity from 1,177 individual neurons and found a significant number of mirror neurons in the front of the brain that were active both when the patients performed the gestures and facial expressions themselves and when they watched someone else performing them.

You might have done something like this yourself if you've ever flung your arms in the air mirroring a sportsperson celebrating victory or found yourself playing air guitar when you were watching a guitarist playing. Your mirror neurons were pulling your strings, so to speak.

## IF YOU CAN, I CAN

Your mirror neurons are active every time you see someone. You can't walk down a street without these cells copying what you see. It's almost like a continuously running video camera in your brain, but one that tries to get you to copy what is being recorded.

Of course, you don't completely mirror everything you see, but you will smile when a person smiles and unconsciously become tense when a stressed or angry-looking person walks past. And your arms will make micro-attempts to move in synch with the arms of the people you are looking at.

Fortunately your mind overrules mirroring the large movements, otherwise you'd be flailing your arms and legs in multiple directions after walking just 20 yards along a busy street. Studies show that you need to focus your attention on a specific body part and its action to activate the appropriate mirror neurons.

The mirroring is mostly subtle, but it can have beneficial consequences. Watching someone exercise, for instance, can actually make us stronger. In a study performed at the University of Modena and Reggio Emilia in 2007,[3] volunteers had a rubber band over their index and third finger and were trained in a simple task of pulling their fingers apart. They had to do 25 repetitions lasting about 3 seconds during each training session, with a 25-second rest between each one. But the key to the experiment was that while one person did the exercise, another person watched them. This was carried out in six sessions over a two-week period.

After the sixth training session the groups were tested. Those who had done the training were 50 per cent stronger, according to a simple force test of their strength. But incredibly, those who had watched the training had also got stronger, by 33 per cent, even though they hadn't technically lifted a finger!

As silly as it may sound, if you aren't the exercise type, you won't go far wrong by sitting in a café at a gym watching everyone else work out. Why not just sip your coffee while keeping your eyes fixed on the man using the cross trainer, willing him to go just that little bit faster. 'That's it. I need to work off that pastry I had for breakfast.'

Of course, you would have to actually pay attention for an entire session, watching each stride and lift, so your coffee might get cold. Supplementing your 'observational training' with a couple of *actual* training sessions would, however, probably find you experiencing fairly large gains in strength and agility, considering how much you had physically exercised.

This would actually be useful for injured athletes. They needn't stay at home feeling frustrated. Getting down to the track or gym every day and watching able athletes train would certainly help them return to training at a higher level than they would otherwise, especially if they were to do it with an awareness of what they were doing.

It would also be useful for any sportsperson who wanted to improve. A golfer studying the motions of great golfers, for example, will prime their own muscles in the same way, so that when they actually come to take their shots, their brain and muscles will be better prepared than they would ordinarily be.

It's not only useful in sport. Musicians can improve by studying the play of great musicians. The key is to place your attention on the mechanical motions.

This powerful phenomenon hasn't escaped clinical attention. In a study performed at University Hospital Schleswig Holstein in Germany, eight moderate to chronic stroke patients were given a four-week course of physiotherapy. Half of them were also invited to spend time every day doing 'action observation', which basically involves watching able-bodied people carrying out simple actions like lifting a cup and turning a water tap on and off.

When the four weeks were up, the patients who had watched the able-bodied people showed much greater improvement than those who had only done the physiotherapy. And crucially, scans showed that some of the damaged parts of their brains were being reactivated.[4]

There is even some early evidence that stimulating mirror neurons might actually be beneficial to Alzheimer's patients. In a pilot study published in 2009,[5] researchers from VU University Amsterdam, the Netherlands Institute for Neuroscience in Amsterdam and the University of Groningen showed either 30 minutes of videos of hand movements to 44 nursing home residents with dementia or a 30-minute documentary for five days each week over six weeks. The residents were tested after the six weeks and then again six weeks later.

The research was based on the fact that hand movements activate mirror neurons in brain areas that are susceptible to Alzheimer's disease.

Crucially, the residents who had watched the hand movements had significantly improved results on an attention test and on face recognition.

So research is now revealing some powerful and beneficial applications of mirror neurons. Looking at actions stimulates our brain and muscles to perform the action ourselves.

When my niece Ellie was a baby she was quite easily distracted and this caused problems at feeding time. My sister Lynn would try to spoon some food into her mouth, but Ellie would quickly turn her face to the side. When Lynn aimed in that direction, Ellie would switch again. Eventually Lynn learned that making 'choo choo' sounds as she moved the spoon around the air like a small aeroplane worked wonders. It would capture Ellie's attention long enough for Lynn to get the food into her mouth.

I remember once watching this scene play itself out. As Lynn slowly moved the spoon in Ellie's direction and Ellie held her mouth open in anticipation, I glanced around to see my partner Elizabeth, my two other sisters Lesley and Kerry, my mum and dad and my nephews Ryan and Jake all focused on Ellie with their mouths open as if Lynn was bringing the spoon to them next. And I had my mouth open too!

As we had watched Ellie open her mouth, our eyes had sent signals to our mirror neurons, which had then sent signals to the brain cells that govern the muscles of the face. And once these cells had been stimulated, they had sent signals to the actual muscles, which had then reproduced the open mouth scene.

The same kind of thing happened when John entered the room full of people talking. The mirror neurons of several people there began the process of copying his facial expressions, body language and mannerisms. And even people who didn't turn to see him enter couldn't escape his presence, because once the people who had seen him changed, people close to them picked up on their new facial expressions and body language.

Rebecca didn't see John entering the room, but Sarah did. Her brain reacted quickly and her negative thoughts about her job were interrupted because her face and body language subtly changed in response to John's. Then she began to share John's emotional state. If a person in a negative train of thought suddenly shifts their body language or facial expressions to reflect a state of happiness or optimism (even if they are pretending), their mental and emotional state changes to reflect their new physical behaviour.

So, Rebecca's facial expression and body language were mirroring Sarah's, but once Sarah's changed, so did Rebecca's, and their conversation shifted to a more positive topic as a consequence.

And even people who didn't see John enter the room and weren't sharing a conversation with anyone who did couldn't escape his presence. If they heard his voice, which also reflected his upbeat, positive, confident state, his mood spread to them.

Have you ever been in a situation where there was a group of people laughing and it brought out smiles in others close by? The process is mostly unconscious. We don't usually have a mental conversation with ourselves where we analyse other people's behaviour and wonder what is going on in their lives to make them so filled with vitality. OK, we do this sometimes! But aside from this, our senses perceive their facial expressions, pupil behaviour and body language and send signals to our mirror neurons, which begin to reproduce the same expressions and body posture and emotions.

It happens so automatically that we're not even aware of it. In one experiment, two people sat opposite each other without saying a word. One was happier than the other. Within two minutes, the less happy person was feeling happier.[6]

If this effect could be shown using computer graphics, you would actually see the less happy person's brain light up to be the same colour as the happy person's. Similarly, in a room full of people you would see the happy colour spread like a wave.

## THE CHAMELEON EFFECT

The way we unconsciously mimic the facial expressions, mannerisms and body language of others has been called the 'chameleon effect'.[7]

It seems this mimicry is related to empathy. People who are more empathetic unconsciously mimic more than those who are less empathetic.

Researchers from Leiden University in the Netherlands tested this by experimentally manipulating a person's liking for another person (usually an actor) to see if it had any effect on their mimicking of that person's behaviour.[8] It did. The results showed that the more we like someone, the more we are likely to mimic them. In fact, several studies have shown this.

On the other hand, it has also been shown that we mimic people less when we don't like them.[9]

In one experiment, volunteers were invited to participate in an ice-cream taste test.[10] Pretending that he was one of the participants, an actor either ate a lot or very little ice cream. The experiment was performed twice. The first time, the actor employed was obese and in the second he had a facial birthmark.

The participants mimicked the person with the birthmark, but didn't mimic the obese person. Obesity carries a social stigma. This suggests that we override our natural tendencies to mimic when we don't want to bond with a person or be like them.

So, we mimic more when we like someone or when we *feel* like someone – when we feel connected to them in some way. Aside from genetics, this is why kids grow up to have the same mannerisms as their parents.

People who practise NLP are familiar with 'mirroring', where we mirror someone's subtle movements, like how and when they move their hands, and even their breathing rate. This helps us to create rapport – that is, to bond with them – and to understand them.

But research shows that it also improves the chances of them liking us. Typical experiments have had two participants performing an irrelevant task, but one of them is an actor planted by the researchers. The actor then intentionally mimics the other person – their breathing, posture, facial movements, mannerisms and even some of their speech. The results show that the person being mimicked likes the actor more than someone not being mimicked does and also has much smoother interactions with them.[11]

Infants do the same thing. Research shows that they also like people who imitate them more, indicating that this capacity is deep-rooted in us.

Incredibly, we even like computer characters (avatars) who mimic us. A 2005 study used virtual reality technology to create an avatar who mimicked some of the head movements of an observer, with a four-second delay so that the participant would not be aware of the mimicry. This was compared with an avatar who made pre-recorded movements of another participant. The avatars who mimicked were rated more positively and as more persuasive, even though the participants in the experiment weren't even aware of the mimicry.[12]

What does this mean for us? Mirroring someone brings us emotionally closer to them in the sense that we like them more and they like us more. And as this occurs, emotional contagion takes place more efficiently. Think of emotions flowing between two people as like an electric current flowing along a wire. When we like someone we share a good conducting wire, a piece of copper for instance. But when we don't like someone, it's like a rusty wire and the emotions don't transmit the same.

Many waiters receive larger tips through a form of mimicry. Research shows that waiters who recite a customer's order back to them get larger tips than those who don't. In a simple experiment published in 2003, for instance, a waitress was either asked to recite a customer's order back to them or not to do so. She got bigger tips when she repeated the order than when she didn't.[13]

Mimicry leads us to a deeper sense of closeness with one another. This was shown in a study where an experimenter conducted a fake marketing study and mimicked the behavioural mannerisms and posture of some of the participants in the experiment. The participants then completed a questionnaire that measured interpersonal closeness and it was shown that those who had been mimicked felt, in general, closer to other people than those who hadn't been mimicked.[14] Mimicking closes the emotional distance between two people.

An extension of this is that if we consciously start to mimic people, they will eventually unconsciously mimic us. For instance, you might copy some of the subtle postures of people in a group. After a while, when you have closed the emotional gap a little, they will unconsciously start to follow your movements. If you then want to raise the mood of the group, all you need to do is introduce some positive facial expressions and body language – maybe a smile from time to time. It's subtle, but effective.

## QUICK OFF THE MARK

As we know, we copy people's facial expressions without ever realizing that we're doing it. A study conducted by scientists from Uppsala University in Sweden showed just how automatic and unconscious this is.[15] One hundred and twenty volunteers looked at photographs of neutral faces on a computer screen. Or so they thought! Actually, a happy or an angry face was flashed onto the screen immediately before the neutral face, but only for 25–35 milliseconds – so fast that the participants couldn't consciously see it.

Nevertheless, their faces reacted. Using a technique called facial EMG, which measures movements of the facial muscles, the scientists recorded tiny facial muscle twitches. Facial EMG is very reliable because it allows us to measure muscle twitches that are smaller and faster than the human eye can recognize. In the experiment, when a happy face was flashed onto the screen, the facial muscle which raises the lips at the sides to produce a smile, known as the *zygomaticus major* muscle, was stimulated, and when an angry face was flashed onto the screen, the *corrugator supercilli* muscle, which knits the eyebrows together in a frown, was activated. (We should really call this the 'super chilly' muscle, since it can be associated with an ice-cold expression. No? Oh well.)

The point is that the participants' faces mirrored those that appeared on the screen automatically and without their conscious awareness. And since emotion is conveyed in facial expressions, a person's mood is transmitted in the same way, and really quickly.

In another study, 17 volunteers had to observe movie clips of actors showing happiness, fear or disgust, or making neutral facial expressions like blowing out their cheeks. They were also asked to imitate the facial expressions so that the researchers could track the regions of the brain that processed the emotions corresponding to these faces.

MRI scans showed activation in the same areas of the brain's emotional regions when the participants made the expressions themselves as when they watched the actors do so. They weren't just mirroring the facial expressions, they were sharing the *emotional state* of the people whose pictures they saw.[16]

Another study specifically examined the facial expressions of disgust.[17] Participants inhaled horrible smells while MRI scans recorded the active areas of the brain. Then they were shown video clips of someone else expressing disgust as they smelled the contents of a glass. When the volunteers watched these clips, the same emotional areas of the brain were activated as when they had actually felt disgusted themselves. Their brains reacted in the same way regardless of whether they actually felt disgust or saw someone else experience it.

In a sense, when we see someone inhaling a pungent smell, our brain thinks we are inhaling it too and reproduces not just the facial expression of the person inhaling but the actual emotion that accompanies that facial expression. It is not just that our brain stimulates the appropriate muscles as we mirror the facial expression (via mirror neurons), but that our emotional areas are also stimulated.

So the mirror neuron system can be considered to contain an emotional part too. And it is not just a fake emotion that we feel. We really do feel the same emotion as the other person.

## 'I FEEL YOUR PAIN'

Studies have shown that the mirror neuron system is highly specific. If you were to watch someone suffering a pinprick to their right hand, then the part of your brain governing your right hand would be activated. And the emotional component of your brain would also be activated. That's how in tune we are with others.

The specificity of the mirror neuron system was shown in a 2004 study where parts of the secondary somatosensory cortex, a brain region that governs specific body areas, were activated whether the subject had their own leg touched or watched someone else having their leg touched.[18]

Just as seeing someone moving activates the brain areas involved in moving, when we see someone being touched or in pain, our brain acts as if we are the ones being touched or in pain. We don't physically feel the pain of others, but our brain lights up in the area corresponding to where the pain is located.

The mirror neuron system involved in this reaction contains three main sections:

a sensory part, which focuses on the specific area where we see the pain, touch or movement

a motor (movement) component, which stimulates similar movement in us if it's a movement we're looking at

an emotional (affective) part, which processes the amount of pleasure or displeasure we see. This part is involved in the processing of empathy. It is especially active when we see someone in pain. We literally feel for them.

All of this has been concluded from exciting research that gives the impression that our mind doesn't just stop at the boundaries of our skin, but in a way actually reaches out and experiences the world through other people's senses.[19]

A 2005 study, for instance, showed participants images of a knife cutting someone's hand or a foot stuck in a door.[20] MRI scans showed that the hand or foot sensory areas of participants' brains had been activated on viewing the pictures. But so had the regions involved in the emotional experience of it. In a very real sense, when we see someone having their hand cut or getting their foot stuck in a door, we are sharing everything except the physical pain.

Similarly, a 2007 study had volunteers watch videos of acupuncture needles being inserted into parts of a person's body, including the mouth, hands and feet. Again, the brain regions activated were the sensory ones governing the exact point of the needle jab and the emotional ones.[21]

How much the emotional regions of the brain are activated when we see another person in pain depends upon how much empathy we feel for them. In a 2004 study, volunteers received a small electric shock and also watched a loved one receive the shock. As with other studies, the same brain areas were affected each time regardless of whether the participants received the shock themselves or saw their loved ones receive it. But the level of activation in the emotional areas was dependent upon empathy. According to a questionnaire that rated empathy, the people who scored highest also had the most active emotional centres of the brain when they watched a loved one suffer the electric shock.[22]

We don't even have to see a person being shocked to feel their pain. The pain is contagious even when we just see their face. In one study, conducted at the University of Pennsylvania, McMaster University and the University of Northern British Columbia, volunteers viewed either neutral facial expressions or grimaces of pain. When they saw the pain in the faces, the regions of their brains involved in the emotional experience of pain were activated. As far as the brain was concerned, they were feeling the pain that they saw in the faces of others.[23]

## EXTENSIONS OF THE SELF

Slight variations or cross wiring in the mirror neuron system show just how much our mind seems to be able to reach out and sense the world through others. A condition known as synaesthesia causes some of our senses to be blended together. For instance, in the common form, known as grapheme-colour synaesthesia, people with synaesthesia (synaesthetes) see numbers or letters in different colours. The number one might be red, for instance whereas two might be blue.[24] Together with the mirror neuron system, synaesthesia shows we really can feel what others feel.

This was demonstrated in a 2005 study where scientists at University College London studied 'patient C', who had a condition known as vision-touch synaesthesia, where the senses of vision and touch blend together.[25] When 'C' saw people being touched on the face or neck, the face or neck area of her own brain that gave an actual physical sense of touch (the primary somatosensory cortex) was activated and she physically felt the touch herself.

You might think of it as a highly sensitive or exaggerated sense of touch – so exaggerated and extended that 'C' could actually experience more of the world through others. The scientists reported that she had an overactive mirror system for touch. And she had experienced it since childhood, so assumed that everyone felt each other's touch.

Usually it's just an emotion that's contagious rather than a physical experience. But we all have the basic architecture in our brains for this type of phenomenon. It was just a little more active in 'C'.

Synaesthesia, however, is more common than we might think. It is estimated that as many as 1 in 23 people in the world have some form of it. Some people can smell colour and even perceive emotion from paintings. Some even see numbers as distances – for example, the year 1999 might appear farther away than 2010. Synaesthesia has been used to explain the extraordinary abilities of some people with autism spectrum disorders to be able to recite 'pi' (3.1415... etc) to thousands of decimal places. Some report seeing the number series as changing landscapes.

One recently reported form of synaesthesia might even explain the 'psychic' ability to see auras. Many people have reported that they can see coloured hues around people. The scientific community has largely dismissed this kind of anecdotal report, but new evidence suggests that the ability is real.

During a 2010 presentation at the Society for Neuroscience Annual Meeting, Luke Miller presented results from his research team, led by eminent neuroscientist Vilayanur Ramachandran. They had studied a 23-year-old male, known in the study as 'RF', who had Asperger's syndrome.[26]

When RF was a child he had difficulty perceiving people's emotions, which is typical of children with autism spectrum disorders. So his mother asked him to try to match the emotions with a colour. After a few years, this practice actually evolved into a full-blown ability to see 'auras of colour' around people. And, according to RF, they changed with different emotions, which is something that some psychics say they experience.

Ramachandran's team hypothesized that RF's ability to see colour around people might be due to a link-up between the area of the brain responsible for the perception of colour, known as V4, and an area known as the insula. The insula is part of the empathy area of the brain and is active when we see someone in pain or see an emotion in someone's face or body language. With this link to V4, in a sense RF's mirror neuron system expanded to include colour perception. Therefore, when his brain detected facial expressions, rather than only stimulate the insula so that he could feel the emotion, this stimulated his sense of colour perception too and so he saw coloured auras around people.

Seeing colours around people due to synaesthesia doesn't necessarily prove that psychic auras exist as a physical emanation. But it does suggest that some people really can perceive others' emotions in colour.

Setting aside synaesthesia for now, much of the research into facial expressions and mirror neurons has used facial expressions of pain because they are relatively easy to reproduce reliably in laboratory conditions. But, as we know, the emotional regions of the brain aren't activated to the same extent in everyone. The level of activation depends on our capacity for empathy. They more we feel for others, the more our brain shares their pain.

This has been demonstrated in a number of studies. In a 2007 study, scientists at Helsinki University of Technology not only showed that when 42 participants watched pain in the faces of chronic pain sufferers the brain's emotional areas of the pain matrix (which includes the insula) were activated, but that they were activated in proportion to the amount of pain that they thought the person was experiencing.

And just as with the electric shock study mentioned earlier, prior to viewing the faces the volunteers had filled out questionnaires designed to measure empathy. And the results showed that the degree of brain activation correlated with the empathy ratings. The volunteers who had the highest empathy ratings had the greatest brain activation.[27]

If you think about it, our brains have had a lifetime to forge strong bonds between our facial expressions and the emotions that accompany those expressions. Think of it like the conditioning of Pavlov's dogs. Each time Pavlov started a metronome ticking, he brought food for the dogs and they would salivate. Their brains eventually created strong connections between the sound of the metronome, food arriving and involuntary salivating. Once these connections were established, all it took was for Pavlov to set the metronome ticking and the dogs would automatically salivate.

In the same way, several years of experiencing facial expressions and the emotions we feel at the time of seeing them will create strong connections in our brain that will connect the facial expression with the emotion. So when we see the same expression on another person, it is just like Pavlov starting the metronome, only we don't salivate (unless of course we're watching someone eat a tasty meal or a big slice of cake!), but experience the emotion that our brain has associated with that expression. And the more empathetic we are, the more emotion we feel. So when we see a person suffering, we experience emotional suffering in accordance with our level of empathy.

This sort of Pavlovian classical conditioning has occurred since we were born. But the roots run much deeper. The ability is actually genetically wired in us, as we will learn later.

## BODY LANGUAGE

As some research indicates, emotional information is not only transmitted though facial expressions, but body language too. If a person turns and runs from something, we can get a fairly clear idea that there is something to be afraid of. But the full picture of emotional contagion involves a whole range of subtleties of movement and gesture. It even involves vocal tone. We speak to babies with softer, higher-pitched tones, for instance. All or any one of those individual modalities is capable of transmitting emotion.

Facial expressions, body language and voice as transmitters of emotion have been studied by researchers at the Rudolf Magnus Institute of Neuroscience at University Medical Center, Utrecht, in the Netherlands. In a 2007 report[28] they showed that when people viewed bodily expressions representing 'happy' or 'fearful' and also face–voice combinations of the same, the facial muscles of happiness (*zygomaticus major*) and fear (*corrugator supercilli*) were stimulated, as measured by facial EMG.

The first part of the study involved 13 participants who viewed various combinations of faces paired with sentences read in either a happy or fearful tone. Facial EMG analysis revealed that happy faces activated the *zygomaticus major* muscles and fearful faces activated the *corrugator supercilli* muscles.

Then audio was added. Happy faces were shown together with a sentence spoken in a happy tone or a sentence spoken in a fearful tone, or the other way around. Facial EMG reading showed that the participants' *zygomaticus major* muscles were activated when they saw happy faces paired with happily spoken sentences and not when a happy face was paired with a fearfully spoken sentence, and the same was true for the fearful faces. Voice was significant in the transmission of emotion. It had the capacity to drown out the emotion presented on the face.

In the second part of the experiment, 13 participants were shown pictures of bodies in either a happy or fearful posture with the faces greyed out. Facial EMG readings again showed activation of the *zygomaticus major* for happy postures and activation of the *corrugator supercilli* for fearful postures.

This showed that we detect, and therefore absorb, emotions from people's body language and speech as well as from their faces.

## 'I HEAR YOU'

Mirror neurons also extend to hearing. When we hear the actions of another person, say walking or playing the piano, our brain thinks we are actually doing the same.

Have you ever found yourself keeping the beat with your fingers when you hear music? It's your mirror neurons stimulating your muscles.

A study of concert pianists examined the brains of five female musicians with an average of 19 years' playing experience and five female non-musicians while they listened to a short piano piece. It turned out that there was activation in both the auditory and motor (movement) areas of the brain when they listened. In other words, their finger areas were stimulated as if they really were playing the piano they were listening to.

Interestingly, there was much higher activation in the musicians than in the non-musicians, suggesting that the auditory and motor areas are neuroplastic, i.e. they actually grow in a similar way to a muscle.[29]

In another study, scientists at the University of Parma in Italy showed that listening to someone talking about hand or foot movements stimulated the areas of the brain that governed these movements.[30] Even listening to a person counting activates areas of the brain that govern finger muscles, as if we are counting on our fingers.

And as strange as it sounds, research shows that hearing a person talking activates our tongue muscles. My partner Elizabeth, who is an actress with a particular expertise in different accents, says her tongue actually starts moving when she hears a new accent, as if she is mirroring it and trying to reproduce it.

And just as with seeing a person in pain, the auditory mirror neuron system is also affected by the level of empathy. In one study, volunteers listened to actions and the same brain areas were activated as when they did the actions themselves. When they listened to hand movements, for example, the hand area was activated, and when they listened to speech, the tongue area was activated. And those who scored highest on the empathy scale had the highest brain activation.[31]

## PUPILS SAY IT TOO

The pupils of our eyes also transmit emotional information. Studies show that they adjust in size to match those of the people we are looking at.[32] This, too, involves mirror neurons.

In a 2008 study, 27 men viewed a number of photographs of unfamiliar female faces, many of which had been altered on Photoshop to have pupils that were either 30 per cent larger or 30 per cent smaller. Viewing the faces with large pupil sizes substantially increased amygdala activation in the participants' brains.[33] The amygdala is also part of the mirror neuron system.

The fact that larger pupils impact men's brains might be unconsciously why women draw attention to their eyes. They actually make their eyes appear bigger by applying eye make-up.

✳✳✳✳✳

When we watch the world go by it can be like watching a movie. We share the lives of the actors. We feel their emotions. We can tell when they are hurt and we feel sad for them. Our body even expresses their emotions with tears, changes in our own heartbeat, body chemistry, immune function and even blood flow to our muscles.[34] And the closer we are to people, the stronger these effects – the stronger the contagion.

In one sense, every person we see is an extension of ourselves. We have our five physical senses, but emotional contagion and mirror neuron research suggests that we also have an extended sense, one that allows us to share some of the experiences of everyone we see. We feel what they feel as if their body is sensing the world for us, almost as if it is one of our own arms or legs. Our brain processes some of their physical and emotional experience as if it were our own. So we share the lives, emotions and experiences of those around us.

As Nietzsche writes, 'A good writer possesses not only his own spirit but also the spirit of his friends.'[35] Our friends are part of us and we are part of them and we 'infect' each other with our emotions.

But it's not just emotions that travel from person to person – yawns are contagious too!

# CHAPTER 2

# ONE GOOD YAWN DESERVES ANOTHER

**'Tis now the very witching time of night,
When churchyards yawn
and hell itself breathes out
Contagion to this world.'**
William Shakespeare

Have you ever yawned after seeing another person yawn? It is unstoppable once it has started. It is a part involuntary response and starts in the brain.

That yawning is contagious is not a new idea. It has been known about for centuries. On 9 March 2005 the popular TV programme *MythBusters* set out to examine it and ended up proving it. In one study, after watching a video of a person yawning, more than 50 per cent of people yawned too.[1]

We can even be infected by someone yawning on the phone. Many of us only need to *think* of a person yawning to start yawning ourselves. In fact, there have been experiments where merely thinking about yawning has been used to induce yawning so that it can be studied.[2]

And, as unsurprising as it might seem, some people yawn after just reading about yawning. If you're anything like a sizeable percentage of the population, you'll be yawning right now.

But don't go to sleep – you've got more interesting reading to do!

## WE ARE NOT ALONE

We're not the only ones who find yawning contagious. In a 2006 study, 22 stumptail macaques were either shown videos of yawning or of a control open-mouth expression. The monkeys yawned much more during and after watching the yawning clip than when they watched the control clip.[3]

Yawning is also known to be contagious in chimpanzees. In a 2004 study, six adult female chimpanzees either watched videos of other chimpanzees yawning repeatedly or simply opening their mouths (as a control).[4] Two out of the six chimpanzees then yawned significantly more. Although it was not all six, it did indicate that yawning contagion exists in chimpanzees.

Chimpanzees even catch yawning from animated characters. In a 2009 study, 24 chimpanzees were shown 3D computer animations of chimpanzees yawning or making an open-mouth expression that wasn't yawning. As with the videos of real chimpanzees, significantly more chimpanzees yawned after seeing the animated character yawn than after the control expression.[5]

Have you ever caught a yawn from your dog? Or has your dog ever caught one from you? Yawning has even been shown to jump the species barrier. In a 2008 study, psychologists at the University of London conducted an experiment in which 29 dogs (12 females and 17 males) observed either a human yawning or making other mouth movements (as a control). After seeing the yawning, 21 of the 29 dogs also yawned, but not one single dog yawned after seeing a control mouth movement.[6]

## A QUESTION OF EMPATHY

Research into the contagiousness of yawning suggests that it has something to do with empathy. The ability to feel empathy actually seems to be required in order to be susceptible to yawning contagion.[7]

Yawning is contagious to dogs, then, because they are very empathetic. I read a very interesting article in the *Observer* magazine on 31 October 2010 by a journalist-turned-dog-rescuer.[8] He had had a bad fall and, being injured, was worried about the usual reaction of his dogs as he approached his house. Normally they would welcome him by barking and jumping all over him. But that day they could tell that he was injured and instead they quietly walked him back to the house. Then they took it in turns to lick his head while the others rested their heads on his shoulder. He remarked that you wouldn't read about this kind of thing in an academic journal or book, but it happened.

Those dogs were clearly displaying empathy and many dog owners could probably testify to experiencing something similar.

Empathy in other animals has also been linked to contagious yawning. In a 2009 study, 3,229 yawns were recorded from gelada baboons. The premise of the study was that empathy was strongest in similar or socially close individuals, so if yawning was related to empathy then contagious yawning would also be greater in similar or socially close individuals. Indeed, after studying all of the yawns the researchers found that contagious yawning was more common between baboons who were socially closer or showed more bonding with one another.[9]

The empathy link has since been confirmed by a brain study. This showed that when people viewed yawning, a part of the prefrontal cortex known as the ventromedial prefrontal cortex was activated. This part of the brain is believed to be involved in the regulation of emotion and empathy. The researchers pointed out that the activation was independent of the mirror neuron network, so, in other words, contagious yawning is not mimicry but empathy.[10] We don't yawn because we are mirroring facial expressions; we yawn because we feel for each other.

Other research has also shown that contagious yawning is independent of mirror neurons. In a 2005 study of the brain, when volunteers watched videos of yawning there was no activation of a key area of the mirror neuron system.[11]

Another link with empathy came in a 2007 study that showed that yawning was not as contagious in autistic children. In the study, 24 children with autism spectrum disorder, who typically tend to show less empathy, were compared to 25 normally developing children as they watched video clips of yawning or control mouth movements. The autistic children did not yawn as much as the normally developing children after viewing the clips.[12]

Another study of 120 children, including 28 with autism spectrum disorders, found the same thing, and also that the contagiousness of yawning differed with different variants of autism. The children with a milder variant of autism, who were able to experience some empathy, caught yawning more easily.[13]

Since yawning is linked to empathy, contagious yawning depends upon the emotional distance between people rather than the physical distance. Although we are still likely to yawn when we see a stranger yawn, we are more likely to yawn when there is emotional closeness.

Another way to think of contagious yawning is by considering the view that we yawn to gain oxygen. Maybe this is *why* it triggers empathy, especially in bonded individuals, as it is our unconscious mind recognizing a person needing oxygen and therefore 'in distress'. As I pointed out in my book *Why Kindness Is Good for You*, we're genetically wired to be kind. When we see a person in distress, we're moved to help.

Whatever the reason behind it, contagious yawning certainly demonstrates a connection between two people.[14] Something one person does causes an automatic neural reaction in another person. It's almost as if one person's mind touches that of another person, or people are somehow connected to each other by an invisible cord. As one person tugs on the cord, others, especially those with some form of emotion bond with that person, unconsciously feel the pull and move in response.

# CHAPTER 3

# EMOTIONAL CONTAGION STARTS EARLY

**'Children are like wet cement. Whatever falls on them makes an impression.'**
Dr Haim Ginott

Emotional contagion is an inbuilt thing and has been studied in infants for a number of years.

Newborn babies have a well-developed capacity to sense the emotional states of other babies.[1] One crying infant can set off a wave of crying in a hospital ward.

Babies pick up the emotions of their parents too. Much of this presumably occurs via the mirror neurons that the baby is born with, which cause it to imitate the facial expressions it sees. The process starts before the infant has the awareness to consciously try to copy the parent. It's an automatic thing.

This was suggested by a 1983 study where a woman put on a happy, sad or surprised face in front of newborn infants. When she put on the happy face, the infants' lips widened more.

Her sad face brought about more pouting lips. When she did 'surprise', the infants had wider open mouths.[2]

A 1988 study of newborns in rural Nepal showed the same thing, indicating that the capacity is not learned, nor is it specific to North American or European children, who have been the most studied.[3] Nadja Reissland of Oxford University observed 12 newborns in rural Nepal during their first hour postpartum while a model made lip movements (widened and pursed). Even at this early age, the babies frequently moved their lips in accordance with the model.

It's easy to think that the infants just do this because the adult is doing it and that's all there is to it. But what we're seeing is emotional contagion at work. Once we move our faces, emotions arise whether we're doing so because we're thinking about something or because we're around someone else who is moving their face and we're unconsciously mirroring them.

My friend Bryce has the happiest baby in the world, he tells me. She's called Alyx. When she was tiny, Bryce was told that she wouldn't smile in response to him or his partner Allyson because babies couldn't see very far. So they made a point of smiling right up close to her, and they did it a lot. Now she smiles pretty much all the time and brings out the same in her proud parents.

A 1972 study showed that babies also match the sounds they make to the frequency of those they hear around them.[4] Ten seven-month-old infants were played recordings of vowel sounds with either a high or low pitch. The researchers found that the infants modified the number of sounds they made and also the frequency of their vocalizations depending on the frequency of the sound they heard.

Infants do generally match facial expressions, pupil size, voices and movements that they see and hear. They are far more aware than we assume, even if it is not in a fully conscious way. The environment we create around them matters. If we feel something and show it in our behaviour, their nervous system feels it too. In a way, a baby can sense some of the world around it through its parents.

## EMOTIONAL CONTAGION IN THE WOMB

This even starts in the womb. As foetuses, we can hear our mother's voice and other voices.[5] Research has shown that the sound level gets filtered a little but there is almost perfect transmission of the intonation.[6] We start to respond to sound during the third trimester, from around 28–30 weeks, or even earlier, if a 2010 report is anything to go by. Using 3D and 4D scanning equipment, a foetus was captured on film by Professor Stuart Campbell, former head of obstetrics and gynaecology at King's College and St George's hospitals in London, smiling at just 17 weeks.[7]

By almost full term (36–40 weeks), foetuses can discriminate between a vowel and a consonant. A 1987 study showed that a foetus could distinguish between 'babi' and 'biba', as indicated by changes in heart rate.[8]

Other studies involving pregnant women in their third trimester have found that when 'ee' and 'ah' sounds are repeatedly played over their abdomen, the foetus's heart rate decreases.[9]

Almost full-term foetuses can even distinguish between male and female voices. When a man and a woman say the same sentence, the foetus's heart rate changes.[10]

Foetuses also recognize their mother's voice and are able to distinguish it from other voices. In a 2003 study, scientists played voice sounds from both the mother and a stranger to the mother's tummy for three two-minute periods. The heart rate of the foetus changed according to whether the mother or the stranger spoke.[11]

Couples arguing regularly might not realize the effect they are having on their baby or foetus. They might think, 'It's just a baby, it doesn't understand.' But it may be that it understands better than they think. Its neurology, emotional circuits and nervous system may understand all too well the anger and rage they are throwing at each other.

Increased stress hormones in a woman while pregnant will condition the growing child to have an elevated stress response. But its growth and development will also be affected. Studies of premature infants shine a light on how a foetus might respond to differences in its environment. Although studies haven't been done on the effects of anger and rage on a growing foetus, it has been shown that a positive environment for the premature infant has a positive effect upon its growth. Consequently, a negative environment will most likely have a negative effect.

A 2008 study examined the effect of the mother's voice on 14 stable premature infants of 31 to 34 weeks' gestation. Recordings of the voices were played to the infants. They moved less and were more awake when they heard the sounds.[12]

Presumably, the mothers' voices were gentle. Babies recognize human voices regardless of what we say, but how we say it does matter. Infants respond more when speech is directed at them in the playful tones most adults use when speaking to a baby than when two adults are talking amongst themselves. And they will respond even while they sleep, or at least their brain will respond.

In a 2007 study, the mothers of 20 full-term infants read a sample of *Little Red Riding Hood* either to their baby (infant-directed speech, i.e. playful tones directed at the baby) or to another adult (adult-directed speech, i.e. conversational speech between two adults). This meant that their tone, intonation and vocal stressors were different in each case.

The prefrontal cortex of the babies' brains – the part behind the forehead area that is associated with positive feelings and emotional balance in children – showed significantly greater activation with the infant-directed speech than with the adult-directed speech. Adult-directed speech, in fact, didn't activate the prefrontal cortex at all, which the researchers suggested might mean that adult-directed speech doesn't provide emotional stimulation to a baby.[13]

What research of this type shows is that in hearing our voices, foetuses and infants detect the emotions carried by them and share them too. Our emotions are not nearly as private as we think.

And infants have a preference for their own mother's voice, presumably because they have become familiar with it while in the womb. This preference was experimentally demonstrated in research in 1980.[14] The study involved ten newborn infants and their mothers. The mothers were asked to read Dr Seuss's *And to Think That I Saw It on Mulberry Street* and this was recorded to be played to their babies. The babies had a non-nutritive nipple placed in their mouths and earphones carefully placed on it. Instruments were used to record their sucking behaviour, which came in bursts. The scientists recorded the typical sucking behaviour and then introduced the sounds.

The babies swiftly learned that if they sucked in a particular way, either starting or stopping a burst of sucking, that it would activate their mother's voice, and if they sucked in different ways they would activate a different woman's voice. They actually learned to produce their own mother's voice and they did it much more often than producing the other woman's voice, showing that they preferred their mother's voice to that of a random female.

*****

There is no doubt that foetuses and infants detect sounds and feel the emotions of those around them. So how we act around infants and pregnant women matters. We do not stop at the boundary of our own skin. Our thoughts, words, actions and emotions filter outwards and inform and infect those around us.

So the next time you offer up your seat on the tube or bus to a pregnant woman, you can take pleasure in knowing that the baby is benefitting too.

## SPONGE BOB

Perhaps unsurprisingly, children also absorb adults' emotions. This can be good when the adult is enjoying interacting with the child, but sometimes it's not such a good thing, especially if the adult is angry. Children are highly emotionally sensitive and will adopt similar facial expressions and emotions and express themselves in the same way as their parents.

This was shown in a 2004 study of 159 children.[15] Their mothers' expressions of negative emotion were correlated with the children's negative facial expressions while watching a distressing film of about three minutes length about a child's parents who were arguing. A child's expressivity will affect its social functioning later in life, so if a parent's negative expressivity can inform the child's expressivity, then the sins of the parent, so to speak, are passed on to the child. A child's social functioning in later life can be a consequence of the parent's emotional issues.

Anger can be particularly contagious to children. Some studies show that many children who see adults behaving angrily towards each other will themselves become aggressive towards other children.[16] This aggression isn't intellectual rebellion; it is that the child is feeling the same emotions as the parents.

Think of how the wave of anger emanates from the adult like wispy strands of invisible fog, causing harm to everything that it falls upon... Most of us have no idea of the consequences of what we say and do and how many people they can affect. Anger is like a heavy stone thrown into one side of a pond that sends a frog falling off a lily pad at the other side.

Marital conflict can have consequences for children's immediate and long-term health, being associated with poorer health later in life.[17] It is believed that this is because it alters the child's stress response and cardiovascular, endocrine and neurotransmitter functioning.

Children whose parents have high levels of marital conflict and are highly negative have been found to have higher levels of stress hormones in their urine than children from typical households.[18]

The seeds of many divorces (not all of course) are sown by toxic emotions which are often expelled around the children with little awareness of the effect it has on them. One study of 17,110 children whose parents had divorced showed they had poorer academic performance, more behavioural problems and a greater risk of asthma than children whose parents were together.[19]

In another study, conducted at Brandeis University, it was found that 4,242 middle-aged adults whose parents had divorced before they were 17 had higher levels of acute and chronic health problems.[20] The men, in particular, had poorer-quality relationships and lower self-acceptance (compassion) and their rates of depression were almost double the normal rate.

Ultimately, these health problems are also a predictor of lifespan.

Of course, these studies are summations of large numbers of children and families. Not all divorces or separations have the same consequences. But what the studies do indicate is that these are the consequences in a lot of families.

It's not just the contagiousness of the adults' emotions that cause these negative effects in the children. Many conflicts also lead to poorer parenting, especially if the single parent has to work extra hours and sees their child less, which in turn may have a knock-on effect on the child's stress levels and emotional health.

A good-quality marriage or relationship between the parents is best for a child's overall mental, emotional and physical health, both now and in the future. And this not only affects health, but also the child's academic abilities, the quality of its relationships and even its income as an adult, according to studies.[21]

If a couple does have to separate (and let's face it, sometimes that is better for the child, as it would otherwise be soaking up the deep unhappiness of the parents for a much longer time), then the ideal way is to still be friends. I know that is easier said than done, but if the parents' priority is always the children then they should make the effort wherever possible.

Bruce Willis and Demi Moore are a prime example. They seem to be on great terms and I'm sure this is because they want the best for their kids. Some people say it's strange how they can all be seen together (new partners included), but isn't this the ideal scenario if a couple with children decides to separate? I'm sure Bruce's and Demi's children will be incredibly grateful to them in the future.

So often the energy of a couple's conflict can filter through time, touching others for decades to come. Think of the effects on their children's future relationships and what that means for those in those relationships – partners, children.

With all this in mind, how important it is for schoolteachers to be positive and uplifting, or at least to hide any anger while they are in the classroom. Children spend a lot of their day in the presence of their teachers, who are significant adults in their life.

Think back to your favourite teachers. Are they smiling in your memory? Maybe you can hear a lilt in their voice. Many people have good memories of specific teachers because of how they felt in their class. It's easy to think that you felt good because of what the teacher said or did. This is of course true. But their style will have reflected their interest, enthusiasm and emotions while in the class. Do you remember any teachers who could make just about anything sound interesting? Their interest and enthusiasm will have been contagious.

Looking back, I can now see that I studied chemistry at university because two of my chemistry teachers were like that. And I loved maths because one of my maths teachers was like that too. I scored my highest university marks when professors seemed genuinely interested in and enthusiastic about their subject. And similarly a love for sports was kindled in me by two enthusiastic physical education teachers. I have since taught chemistry and maths and been an athletics coach, passing on my teachers' enthusiastic styles in each of these arenas.

## CATCHING DEPRESSION FROM A PARENT

*'A lot of people don't realize that depression is an illness. I don't wish it on anyone, but if they would just know how it feels, I swear they would think twice before they just shrug it.'*[22]

Jonathan Davis

Unfortunately, depression can also be contagious and can spread from an adult to a child or even a foetus, having biochemical effects that can result in elevated foetal activity, slower pre-natal growth and a greater likelihood of prematurity and low birth weight.

The body chemistry of a foetus, in part, resembles that of the mother: it can have elevated cortisol, lower dopamine and serotonin levels, lower vagal tone and elevated right frontal EEG activity, which is associated with withdrawal. Overall, newborn infants of pre-natally depressed mothers are more nervously aroused and less attentive than infants born to non-depressed mothers.[23]

Of course, the infant itself isn't emotionally depressed. It can't intellectually know what that emotion is. But its brain and body chemistry mirror the mother's, causing slower overall growth and responsiveness.[24]

This can have emotional and physical health consequences for the child, as well as behavioural consequences, and even impact the child's risk of depression when it grows into an adult.

None of this is the mother's fault, and mothers should not beat themselves up or feel the least bit responsible if they are depressed. Depression isn't something you choose. It just happens. It's not your fault.

Many depressed mothers actually don't show any signs of depression when they are with their babies or children. The time they spend with them may in fact be the only time they are not depressed.

The research presented here refers to when a mother clearly shows signs of depression while she is with her infant or child.

This can impact how the infants respond to their environment. Infants of depressed mothers are typically less responsive to voices and faces than infants of non-depressed mothers.

In one study of three-month-old infants, those born to depressed mothers responded much less and more slowly to happy faces than those born to non-depressed mothers.[25] This is why post-natal depression needs to be addressed more.

Infants are born with well-developed empathy centres in their brain. Newborns usually respond quickly to the sounds of other babies crying, which is a mark of empathy and has been called an empathetic response. But those born to pre-natally depressed mothers don't respond as much. They are generally less attentive.

In a 2007 study, newborns of depressed and non-depressed mothers were played sounds of their own and other babies' crying. The babies born to the non-depressed mothers showed reduced sucking and decreased heart rate. They were empathizing. But babies born to depressed mothers showed no change in sucking behaviour or heart rate. The researchers suggested that this might predict a lack of empathy as the baby grew into a child.[26]

Indeed, studies of pre-school children of mothers who were pre-natally depressed do find that these children show less empathy, and it has been suggested that lower attentiveness as a newborn might be a precursor to this.

For instance, a 2000 study examined pre-school children of depressed and non-depressed mothers. EEG readings of the children's brains revealed that the children of depressed mothers had greater activation in the right side of their prefrontal cortex, which is associated with greater negative emotion. They also showed less empathy towards the sounds of a crying infant than the children of non-depressed mothers.[27]

The depressed mothers themselves typically stated approval of their children less often and spent less time helping them.

So what else can happen to the infant of a depressed mother as it grows up? Depressed mothers tend to respond more slowly to their babies' vocal sounds than non-depressed mothers. They also make less baby talk.[28] Studies show that as the infants grow up they have an increased risk of developing depression themselves.[29]

And it can be a recurring condition. In a study of 244 adolescents who had been depressed in the past, those whose mother had a history of severe depression had a higher risk of reoccurrence of depression between the ages of 19 and 24.[30]

The increased risk of depression is not only due to emotional contagion. Children observe their mother's behaviour as she interacts with others and also learn from that. For example, the mother might show anxiety in a number of different situations and the child might soak up that anxiety as a direct transmission of emotion, but also learn from the mother how to interact anxiously or fearfully with people.

And it's not only depressed mothers who affect the child. The mother's relationship with the father, which will also depend upon the father's emotional state, will even impact the growing foetus. After birth, the father will also impact the emotional state of the baby. A 2005 study found that depressed mothers did have a greater effect on the mental health of adolescents than depressed fathers, though.[31]

In general the impact of a depressed father has not been researched as much as that of a depressed mother, probably because it is mostly the mother who is the primary caregiver of an infant. But it is likely that where a depressed father is the primary caregiver, the effects will be the same as for depressed mothers.

If a child catches depression, though, it is not always due to a depressed parent. Many things interact, including genetics, the child's environment and nutrition, and its emotional state. But it's important to be aware of emotional contagion as a very real phenomenon. It is through this awareness that we can take steps to prevent it.

I hope this puts into perspective why it is so important for depressed mothers to get all the help they need and for that help to be available to them. It is up to us, as a society, to campaign for this and to vote for politicians who promise to make it a reality.

We must do all that we can to help. We cannot underestimate the importance of a child's health and that of its mother. These can have an impact on all of us.

Children can be at the mercy of their parents' moods. An adult's stress, which can be a consequence of any number of things, from financial worries to marital conflict to worries about their neighbourhood environment, is transmitted to the child, who then carries this into their environment.

What might that environment be? Some parents live in poor high-crime areas that have few support services, and many are forced into single parenthood. This, too, can create lasting consequences for a child.

Studies show that children who grow up in these environments often display increased aggression and violence at school and are more likely to resort to criminal behaviour than children who grow up in more positive environments.[32] The crime risk is higher for boys, but girls tend to get involved in early sexual activity and substance abuse and eventually anti-social behaviour. It's as if the stress in the parents' environment has spread to the child and its environment.

If a person grows up in a high-crime area and perhaps even dabbles in some petty wrongdoing themselves, will they be stuck with that pattern throughout their life? I'd like to think not. This might hold true in a general sense for some, but there are always exceptions. A different adult influence, for instance a good, caring, inspirational teacher, can be an antidote to a difficult environment and have a lasting impression upon a child. A different group of friends can make a big impression too.

## THE FAST TRACK PROGRAM

Some helpful programmes have been devised to target both children and adults who are encountering stressful life situations.

One of these, the 'Fast Track Program', was an American programme where preventative support was given to 445 high-risk first-grade children and their parents who lived in areas of high crime and poverty. The intervention lasted a full 10 years, taking the children from first grade to tenth grade. The children in the programme were compared with a control group of 446 children who didn't receive the help and the results were published in 2008.[33]

In the programme, the children were given positive behavioural and academic support at both school and home, parents were given education in parenting skills, and mentoring was provided for each child by a same-sex, same-race community volunteer:

*'Intervention components focused both on building the child's behavioral and cognitive skills and on changing the patterns of interaction with important people in the child's social environment (family, school, and peers) to promote healthy relationships with peers and adults.'[34]*

Regular two-hour family group meetings were held at the school. Twenty-two sessions were held in the first grade, 14 in the second grade, eight each year from grades 3 to 5, and regular meetings right through to tenth grade. Each session started with a one-hour group meeting for parents and social skills training for the children. Children were then given half an hour's tutoring in reading skills while being observed by their parent(s) and the last half-hour included some parent–child sharing, where they took part in joint activities. The parents learned effective communication and discipline skills, and the groups promoted the building of positive relationships between the family and school.

After the first year the parents reported more satisfaction in being a parent and less use of physical punishment, and overall they felt their parenting had improved. Observers also reported that the parents showed more warmth and positive involvement in their child's life. The children showed more coping and social problem-solving skills and less aggression when provoked. They also performed better academically than children in the control group.

After the third, fourth and fifth years, both the teachers and parents reported significant improvements in the children's behaviour. They were much less aggressive and disobedient.

By the end of grade 9, the intervention was shown to be responsible for preventing 75 per cent of cases of conduct disorder, 53 per cent of cases of ADHD and 43 per cent of all 'externalizing disorder cases'. The authors pointed out that the programme was costly (approximately $6,000 per child per year), but that had to be weighed against the relative cost to society were it not in place.

Imagine we lived in a world where we didn't need to put a cost on things like this. What would it take?

I have presented these results on purpose, as I'd like to see a contagion effect here – the birth and growth of many, many similar programmes around the world in areas where they can be of most help.

Because, after all, isn't it silly that we can learn to become a good driver or a doctor, but there isn't much in place to learn to be a good parent? We're simply expected to know how to do the most important job of all – raising a child to become a responsible, happy adult.

## WHAT CAN WE DO?

As a society, there are many ways we can help with this.

It is crucial, for a start, that help is offered to mothers and pregnant women who are depressed, both for their own health and well-being and that of the child.

Group psychotherapy combined with massage has been shown to be effective in reducing depression in pregnant women. In a 2009 study, for instance, 112 pregnant women who had been diagnosed as depressed received either once-weekly group interpersonal psychotherapy or once-weekly group interpersonal psychotherapy plus once-weekly massage over a period of six weeks. The women in both groups benefitted, although the group who received the massage as well as the psychotherapy had a greater decrease in depression, anxiety and cortisol levels.[35]

An adult who is steady in a child's life can help through providing structure and stability. Having regular contact with a grandparent, for example, helps the child of a depressed parent, especially when there is a strong bond between them and the relationship is warm and nurturing. However, a stable focus might not only be provided by a grandparent, but also by another relative or a teacher at school. It could even come from a community group or church.

Children in foster homes should have a stable figure too – a guide, a confidant, who is always consistent in the child's life.

Whatever their circumstances, it is vitally important that children get all the help that they need. When a parent is treated for depression, for example, doctors might be able to inform the child's school so that the teachers can look out for signs of anxiety or depression and make help available to the child, either through the school itself or by contacting other family members to make them aware of the impact on the child.

## PEER PRESSURE

Among children and adolescents, emotional contagion can play a secondary role to behavioural or social contagion, which is the spread of behaviour from person to person, or from a group to a person. Contagion of this type has been studied for a long time.

Children in a group adjust their attitudes and behaviour to be like their friends, while adolescents typically spend much more time with their friends than with their parents, so tend to be influenced more by their peers. The average adolescent spends about eight hours of the average day communicating with other people, but only spends 8 per cent of that time talking to adults.[36] How many teens do you know who only speak to their parents at breakfast and dinnertime? After dinner, many retire to their bedrooms to do homework, listen to music, talk to friends on the phone or play computer games.

Many adolescents report feeling happier when they are with their friends than when they're with adults, and this is probably why conflict with parents increases during the teenage years, as adolescents push for independence.

Adolescence is also a time when peer pressure intensifies. Peer pressure, a form of behaviour contagion, is more of a conscious contagion than emotional contagion is. It peaks around the age of 14. Adolescents are more susceptible to this type of contagion than younger children because they depend more on their friends.

One study, for instance, showed that exposing middle adolescents (13–16 years) to peers during a risk-taking task actually doubled the amount of risky behaviour they participated in. Among university undergraduates (18–22 years), the risky behaviour increased by only 50 per cent and there was no increase among adults (24 years and older).[37]

Girls, on the whole, are more susceptible to peer contagion than boys, especially when they experience more social anxiety,[38] and a child who is part of the 'in crowd' is also more susceptible to peer contagion.

In a 2007 study, researchers at the University of Western Ontario studied the effects of two different peer groups – popular groups (kids who were thought of as 'cool') and groups of children who were the most liked, which included children who were thought of as 'nice' and 'kind'. The study involved 526 Canadian children from grades 5–8, with an average age of 12. Each child reported on their own deviant behaviour, like stealing or playing truant, and also on their pro-social behaviour. Each child was also asked to list classmates who started fights or excluded other children, and those who were kind to others and classmates they liked the best. Examining the children over a three-month period, the researchers found that they tended to become more similar to their peers during this time but the effect was more pronounced in the popular groups than in the well-liked groups.[39]

When children or adolescents are part of a popular group, they are under greater pressure to conform if they want to stay popular.

Similarly, in a 2006 study, 43 adolescents (16–17 years) used a chat room and believed that they were interacting with others (planted by the researchers) who were either 'high status' or 'low status' and who endorsed aggressive or health risky behaviour. When they believed they were interacting with high-status individuals, the adolescents showed more conformity behaviour, internalization, aggressive and health-risk attitudes and exclusionary behaviour. They wanted to be part of the 'cool' group and would become aggressive and exclude others to do so.[40]

Interestingly, the adolescents with high ratings of social anxiety were influenced equally by both high- and low-status individuals, but those with low social anxiety were only influenced by the high-status peers. When we're socially anxious, we regard any status of person as 'above' us, so we are more easily led by anyone.

In a report in the journal *Developmental Psychology*, researchers Laurence Steinberg and Kathryn C. Monahan of Temple University in Philadelphia wrote:

> 'As individuals begin to sort themselves into crowds, both perceived and actual pressure to adopt the styles, values, and interests of one's friends may intensify... The increased importance of peers leads adolescents to want to alter their behaviour to fit in; because they care more about what their friends think of them, they are more likely to go along with the crowd to avoid being rejected.'[41]

Outside their groups, where they are no longer under the same pressure to maintain their image, adolescents can behave very differently. I was bullied at school when I was 16–17 years old by the 'in crowd', though I came to learn that individually many of that group were nice people. I recall that when I was standing at the bus stop waiting for my bus home at the end of the school day many times one of the bullies would stop and chat to me as if I was a friend. I would enjoy his conversation and felt that he enjoyed mine. But the next day back at school he would participate in the bullying again because that retained his identity as part of the crowd.

## RESISTING PEER PRESSURE

Most of the research on peer pressure has focused on pressure to do anti-social things, like drink alcohol, take drugs, cheat or steal. It has been shown that adolescents are less susceptible to this negative peer pressure when their parents are well-off or when they live in an affluent area that has access to social resources like organized sports or recreation groups. These provide a more diverse source of influences and people and reduce the adolescents' reliance on fitting in with one particular group.

This was shown, for example, in a 2005 study that examined the contagion of aggression in a sample of 504 girls and boys from low-resource inner-city communities or urban communities with moderate resources. One of the findings was that children with greater access to resources were less susceptible to negative peer pressure than children with access to fewer resources, and that children with access to a greater range of different activities were much less susceptible.[42]

You might think of this in a similar way to bacterial immunity. Eating a greater variety of food is associated with greater immunity to pathogens than eating a smaller variety. In a similar way, participating in a greater variety of activities and thus being part of a greater number of groups confers some degree of immunity to negative peer contagion.

Adolescents who don't have many close friends or none at all are also subject to less negative peer contagion, but this is because they tend to be more influenced by their parents.

Some research has also examined peer pressure to do more pro-social things, like doing well in school, saying no to drugs and even remaining a virgin.

Compared with anti-social peer influences, which peak around the age of 14, pro-social influences peak around the ages of 11–12, although, unlike negative influences, which decrease with age, pro-social influences remain at a steady level.[43] So children can catch good behaviour from others and the tendency will stay with them for life.

But although adolescents are under pressure to conform, many are also learning to stand up for themselves. In a 2007 piece of research that assessed 3,600 males, resisting peer pressure was also shown to peak between the ages of 14–18.[44] This is a time when we strive to carve out a sense of independence and to define to ourselves and to the world who we are.

*****

As babies and children, we can be heavily influenced by the emotions of those around us. Later in life we in turn can infect those around us, including our own children. Few of us realize how contagious – and detrimental – our emotions can be.

So, if we are struggling right now, this might be a time to seek help. And if we have overcome struggles, this might be a time to seek out others *to* help, whether within our own family or circle of friends, or even farther afield.

CHAPTER 4

# CONTAGION FROM VIDEO GAMES

## 'It's time to kick ass and chew bubble gum and I'm all out of gum.'
Duke Nukem

When I was growing up, I spent a lot of time outside. My friends and I played football, rounders and 'the Olympic Games' – we ran, jumped and threw. We also played tag, hide and seek and dodgeball. We climbed trees, picked apples and plums, had adventures and camped out. We rode our bikes and created obstacles to ride around and ramps to ride off. We even jumped our bikes over beer barrels that we 'borrowed' from outside the local pub. I jointly held the record of eight. We had to ride really fast down a hill to pick up the speed to clear them.

Nowadays, a large number of children and teenagers spend much more time inside their houses, where they play video games or watch TV.

In the mid-1980s, when I was a teenager, the average amount of time children and teenagers spent playing video games was only four hours a week. But according to a 2008 survey of 1,178 children and teenagers aged between 8 and 18, children in the US at that time averaged 13 hours a week – a greater than three times increase in just over 20 years. And it's even more if we just count boys. They average 16–18 hours game play per week. Girls average nine hours per week.[1]

This might be causing a severe lack of vitamin D, which we get from the sunlight on our skin, making kids susceptible to osteoporosis and depression. But the major concern of a number of parents isn't necessarily that the children are not playing outdoors but that they are often playing violent video games. Parents worry that the violence can be contagious. And they have a right to be concerned.

Fortunately, the impact of violent video games is now being taken seriously. A 2001 report by the US Department of Health and Human Services summed up the concerns. Reviewing a volume of research, it found that exposure to violent TV between the ages of 6 and 11 had more of an impact on later violent behaviour than having parents who were abusive, being part of a broken home, being exposed to anti-social peers or having a low IQ.

In the introductory message, the then secretary, Donna E. Shalala, writes, 'The first, most enduring responsibility of any society is to ensure the health and well-being of its children.'[2]

The debate has been ongoing for several years, but there is now little doubt from research that violent video games – that is, games that show repeated acts of aggression – impact behaviour. In particular, they have been shown to increase aggression, both in behaviour and in thoughts and feelings. The aggression is contagious. Studies have even shown that the games reduce empathy and pro-social behaviour.[3]

Kindness usually starts with empathy. If empathy is dampened, we are slow to act when a person needs help. And this is exactly what many studies find. Once children have hacked the heads off enough 'evil' enemies, they become desensitized to the violence. And the characters in modern video games being so lifelike adds a new dimension of realism to the experience. Thus, kids become desensitized to the actual emotional pain that they see in real life.

In a 2009 study, for instance, 320 college students (160 male and 160 female) played either a violent video game (*Carmaggedon*, *Mortal Kombat*, *Duke Nukem* or *Future Cop*) or a non-violent video game (*3D Pinball*, *Glider Pro*, *Austin Powers* or *Tetra Madness*) for 20 minutes. Afterwards they were asked to fill out a lengthy questionnaire, but it really was of little value. The point was to keep them there while a fight broke out outside the room. This was actually a recording which had been made by actors, although it was made to sound totally realistic:

**Actor 1:** OK, that's it, I don't have to put up with this shit any longer.

*(At this point the students heard a chair crashing onto the floor and some loud bangs on the door of the room they were in. Actually, one of the experimenters was kicking the door.)*

**Actor 2:** *(Groans in pain.)*

**Actor 1:** Ohhhh, did I hurt you?

**Actor 2:** It's my ankle, you bastard. It's twisted or something.

**Actor 1:** Isn't that just too bad?

**Actor 2:** I can't even stand up!

**Actor 1:** Don't look to me for pity.

***Actor 2:*** You could at least help me get off the floor.

***Actor 1:*** You've gotta be kidding me. Help you? I'm outta here. (*Slams the door and leaves.*)

Would the students help? How long would it take them? The experimenter started a stopwatch…

Players of both the violent and non-violent games helped, which was good, although slightly more players of non-violent games helped (25 per cent versus 21 per cent). But crucially, the average time to help in those who had played the non-violent game was 16.2 seconds, but in those who had played the violent game it was 1 minute, 13.3 seconds. They had become desensitized to violence after only 20 minutes of game play.[4]

The same researchers reported another experiment in the same research paper, but this time involving a violent movie. This time, 162 adults saw either a violent movie (e.g. *The Ruins*) or a non-violent movie (e.g. *Nim's Island*) at the cinema. To create a situation where someone needed help, the experimenters faked a scene either before the participants entered the cinema or on their way out at the end where a young woman with a bandaged ankle had dropped her crutches and was struggling to pick them back up again.

Again, the woman was helped in every case, which is good. But how long it took for her to be offered help depended on what type of movie the participants had watched. Those who had watched a non-violent movie and those who were entering the cinema and had not yet seen either type of movie took about the same time to help, which was 5.46 seconds on average. But those who had watched the violent movie took 6.85 seconds to help – 26 per cent longer.

In reference to both studies, the authors wrote, 'The findings ... suggest that violent media make people numb to the pain and suffering of others.'[5]

Interestingly, in the second study, as the number of bystanders increased, there was a longer delay before someone helped the woman. I think that when a lot of people are around, we assume that someone else will help, so we are less likely to take the initiative. This is also evidence of contagion. Since everyone is doing the same, that is, nothing, we conclude that help isn't needed.[6]

People who are injured or being attacked in these situations can break the contagion by picking out a specific person in the crowd and appealing to them personally for help. This immediately places sole responsibility on that person and increases the chances of help being offered.

## VIDEO GAMES IMPACT THE BRAIN AND PHYSIOLOGY

A 2006 study examined the brains of players of violent versus non-violent video games after they were shown violent images to gauge how they would respond. The researchers found that a key area of the brain involved in violence desensitization, known as P300, was turned down in activity in players of violent video games compared to those who played non-violent games. And, unsurprisingly, those who played the violent video games acted more aggressively in a later task than those who played non-violent games.[7]

A 2007 study studied the nervous system after violent video-game play. Two hundred and fifty-seven college students (124 men and 133 women) either played a violent game (*Carmageddon*, *Duke*

*Nukem*, *Mortal Kombat* or *Future Cop*) or a non-violent game (*Glider Pro*, *3D Pinball*, *3D Munch Man* or *Tetra Madness*) for 20 minutes and then watched a 10-minute video containing scenes of real-life violence (courtroom outbursts, police confrontations, shootings and prison fights). Their heart rate and skin conductance (expressions of the autonomic nervous system) were recorded during this time.

The results showed desensitization in the volunteers who had played the violent video games. Seeing scenes of violence will cause a spike in anyone's nervous system (except for psychopaths), but the heart rates and skin conductance of the volunteers who had played the violent games were both lower when they watched the film clips than the heart rates and skin conductance of the volunteers who had played the non-violent games. They weren't just emotionally desensitized in the subjective sense that it's all in the mind – their nervous system actually reacted differently. They were less aroused by real-life violence.[8]

The trouble with this is that what follows neural and physiological desensitization to violence is less inclination to act when someone is in need of help, as the previous studies clearly showed. Part of this is a feeling that people in need are not in as much pain as they appear. With this lessening sense of empathy comes less sense of another's pain, which leads to less compassion and, ultimately, less kindness.

## NOT ALL IT SEEMS?

Some studies have criticized the research showing that violent game play has negative effects. A 2007 study, for instance, pointed out that a number of studies showing the aggressive-inducing effects of being exposed to violent media had only looked at the short-term effects. A meta-analysis (an analysis of the results of several studies) showed that the aggressive effects had not been proven to occur in the long term.[9]

But even if there is no long-term effect, there is certainly a short-term effect, and anyone who has ever been bullied knows that it only takes one aggressive act or hurtful word to leave you feeling upset, anxious or scared for the rest of the day. And the effects of repetitive bullying can last a lifetime.

Other critics have suggested that the people who were aggressive after game play might have been aggressive to begin with and were therefore attracted to playing aggressive games.

More recent studies have addressed these issues. In 2008, research examining children from the United States, which is considered a high-violence culture, and Japan, which is considered a low-violence culture, measured aggression at the start of the study to control for the possibility that people with aggressive tendencies were more likely to play violent video games. Aggression was then measured after three and six months.

The researchers used three different samples of children. One was made up of 181 Japanese children between 12 and 15 years of age, a second of 1,050 Japanese students between the ages of 13 and 18, and a third of 364 US children aged between 9 and 12 years of age. The researchers found that those who played a lot of violent video games showed higher amounts of aggression later on, even after statistically controlling for violent tendencies at the beginning of the study. The children had actually become more aggressive. And the effect was around the same for children in Japan and the United States, although a little less for older children.[10] Young children are more impressionable.

A 2009 study of 295 German adolescents had similar results. Controlling for aggression and hostility at the start of the study, the researchers found that children who played violent video games were more aggressive and hostile 30 months later.[11]

## HOW REAL CAN IT BE?

One of the concerns of parents is that with advances in computer technology, games are becoming so real that kids can be exposed to 'real-life violence' on a scale they wouldn't even see on TV. It's not so bad if what the kids see is total fantasy – part of them knows it's not real. But many violent games reflect aspects of real life.

A 2009 study compared the effects of playing a realistic violent computer game (where 'realistic' meant the probability of seeing that kind of thing in real life) with those of playing an unrealistic computer game or a non-violent game. A total of 74 volunteers (39 male and 35 female) played one of the three games for 45 minutes. The scientists measured aggressive thoughts and feelings four times during the course of the game-playing as well as continuously measuring physiological arousal. The results showed that playing the realistic game stimulated much more aggressive thoughts and feelings and physiological arousal. The unrealistic violent game also increased aggression and arousal, but not nearly as much as the more realistic game.[12]

The more realistic the game, the greater the consequences.

It turns out that engaging in violent game play is also worse than watching violent TV. With a game, we're controlling the characters, so in a way we are the ones committing the violence. This gives an extra dimension of reality compared to merely watching something on TV.

In a 2008 study, a sample of 57 children aged between 10 and 13 either played a violent video game, watched a violent game being played (which would simulate some of the effects of watching violence on TV) or played a non-violent computer game. The boys who had played the violent video games were more aggressive later in the playground than those who had watched the games being played, suggesting that playing violent computer games leads to more aggression than watching violence on TV for boys. There was no measurable change in the girls, suggesting that violent media contagion is stronger in boys than in girls.[13]

It's clear that playing violent video games increases aggression and dampens empathy and helping behaviour. We must also consider the impact on a growing child's sense of right and wrong. Criminals are heroes in some games, for instance. I personally don't think we should be setting this kind of example to our children.

But despite the evidence of the negative impact of violent game play, we must not forget that there are benefits from game playing too, both from violent and non-violent games.

When my nephew Jake was only seven years old I was literally astonished by the speed at which he navigated around the software of his mum's laptop. He opened several programs and flicked between them much more quickly than most adults do. I actually couldn't keep up with what he was doing. Undoubtedly he learned this skill from moving through the many, many screens required to play *Football Manager, Tiger Woods' PGA Tour* and racing car games, all of which require you to select players and cars from several different screens and to save your current position in the league or Grand Prix. I have no doubt that he also learned the hand–eye co-ordination from playing many of the games.

There is a body of evidence that shows increased visio-spatial co-ordination from playing video games. I played computer games a lot more from the age of 14 onwards, when they were first becoming popular, and using computers helped me feel at ease with them, which is important for children in the modern world where computer technology is everywhere.

I confess I played some violent games, although they were not on the same scale of realism as those of today. I played karate games and watched karate films and fantasized about beating up dozens of ninja assassins. Well, I am male! I also played games that spilled blood and gore. But I never became violent. In fact, other than a few light skirmishes when I was a young teenager, I have never raised a hand to anyone. I think it depends upon the amount of time spent on these games. If more time is spent in a more positive environment then it's OK, I think.

I also taught myself programming using an Acorn Electron computer and even wrote a few games for it – my own versions of space invaders and racing cars, even though they had block graphics. Technology can now be used to create lifelike animations that can positively tug on our heartstrings. The human features of such animations are often exaggerated, but this can increase empathy and emotional transmission, especially if it's a big set of sad eyes. Who didn't cry at *Bambi*?

In 1981, two of Disney's original animators, Frank Thomas and Ollie Johnson, wrote that for characters to display emotion, animators had to 'clearly' and 'unambiguously' show the emotion and it had to be exaggerated to communicate it.[14]

Animation can feel as real as watching a movie with real people, and in light of the evidence of emotional contagion presented so far, animators now have a real opportunity to inspire, to transmit positive emotions and behaviour, and even to help children and adults alike develop a sense of empathy and moral responsibility rather than aggression and hostility.

# CHAPTER 5

# TRANSMITTING EMOTIONS

**'The expression a woman wears on her face is far more important than the clothes she wears on her back.'**
Dale Carnegie

Harry gave a speech. It was brilliant. At times the audience was inspired, at other times sad, as he recounted some of the painful memories from earlier in his life. Everyone listening was with him right through to the end. It was almost as if he was speaking directly to each and every person.

When someone expresses emotion, we feel that emotion. It is contagious. We see this for ourselves when a great speaker lifts us. But it has also been tested experimentally.

In a 2000 study, for instance, participants listened to an actor give a speech in either a happy, sad or neutral voice. When they rated their own emotions after the speech they turned out to be congruent with the tone of the actor's speech – that is, when he spoke in happy tones, they felt happy; when he spoke in sad tones, they felt sad.[1]

In any group – friends, family members or even teams in a business environment – emotional contagion is highly important, although little known or understood. Charismatic leaders are good transmitters of emotion and an entire team may rally around such a person, sharing not only their vision but their conviction to get the job done properly.

Within a group of people, emotions pass from person to person so that the emotions of the group will gradually tend towards an average, but it is the most expressive people who actually set the emotional tone that the others gravitate towards.[2] If you put an expressive person alone in a room with an inexpressive person, it's a fairly good bet that the expressive person will transmit their mood to the inexpressive person and not the other way around.

This was actually first shown in a 1981 study[3] undertaken with 27 highly expressive people and 54 inexpressive people, where three volunteers were placed in each room and asked to allow their minds to wander for two minutes. Unbeknownst to the volunteers, the researchers had ensured that they consisted of one highly expressive person and two inexpressive people. For the two-minute period they were allowed to look at each other but not to speak. Naturally, when a person's mind wanders, their facial expressions, even though only slight, indicate the emotions they are feeling, with tugs on the *zygomaticus major* muscle (indicating happy feelings) and tugs on the *corrugator supercilli* (indicating negative feelings).

When the two-minute period was up, the volunteers were asked how happy, bored or even frightened, anxious or angry they felt. The results showed that most of the inexpressive people had picked up on the mood of the expressive person in the room and, even within two minutes, were feeling some of the same emotions. And it was even more obvious if the expressive person was in a bad mood!

A 1991 study found the same thing. Everyone could transmit happiness, but expressive people were much better at transmitting aggression, sadness, anxiety and even fatigue.[4]

On the plus side, when you're happy and you show it, you make other people happier. Either that or clap your hands! When you're happy and you don't show it, when you internalize the feelings, then people don't pick up on it as much.

This is common sense, but knowing *how* it happens gives us some tools that we can use. Expressive people, for instance, need to learn to manage their negative thoughts and emotions better, lest they infect those around them.

It might be that people in residential care homes infect each other with tiredness. And the same might be true in hospitals. Or anywhere else, for that matter. Have you ever felt exhausted around people who seem tired or energized around people who are always on the go?

As we learned in the first chapter, stroke patients who were merely observing able-bodied people recovered faster than those only receiving physiotherapy. And as Dr Patch Adams has shown us, laughter and joy can be infectious and lift the spirits of people in hospital wards and care homes.

People in care homes or hospitals with a dispiriting atmosphere might actually be better off at home, if sufficient care could be made available. Or perhaps more could be done in these places to raise the mood of residents. With better mood comes better recovery.

What about in relationships? The closer two people are, physically and emotionally, the greater the likelihood of emotional contagion. So what do you do if you're an expressive person and you're in a relationship?

We need to be more responsible in what we express, especially if what we're expressing is complaints. If you feel like a moan, think for a minute. Do you really want to dwell on all that negative stuff, knowing that your loved one might end up feeling it too? If you're quite expressive (or even if you're not), how about practising more positive behaviour, maybe doing a little self-improvement work on yourself, so that what you project is actually something more positive, like happiness, confidence or serenity? Wouldn't that be a nice gift to your loved one?

Of course, it is easier said than done. And sometimes our loved ones would like nothing more than to let us offload our worries and frustrations in their presence. So this is just something to be aware of.

When I first did the 'Complaint Free Challenge', a challenge to go 21 days without a single complaint, moan, criticism or unfair judgement, described in the book *A Complaint Free World* by Will Bowen, the biggest thing I noticed was that those closest to me seemed happier.

I am mostly a very positive, optimistic person, and usually fairly expressive and energetic with it, and I don't think that I complain very much. In the challenge, each time you complain, moan, criticize or unfairly judge, you have to go back to day 1 and start over again. I didn't think I'd have to go back even once. But it actually took me around four months. I honestly thought it would be a breeze. But it wasn't as easy as I thought. It can be a *real* challenge, especially when you get to 15 days and have to start over again, only to get to 17 days and then start over once more. That's a whole month and you've only complained twice!

Even though I didn't consider myself a moaner, I learned that when I did moan I was pretty good at it. In fact I reckon I could have won a medal if moaning was an Olympic sport. On the occasions I did moan, I put as much energy into feeling sorry for myself as I did into positivity. And what must that have been like to live with? 'Poor Elizabeth,' I thought. When I cut down on complaining, she definitely seemed happier.

What if you're in a relationship where you're both expressive or both inexpressive? It can have consequences – a breakdown in communication as you fail to understand each other. Shouting and silence can, I suppose, be strangely similar.

One of the benefits of emotional contagion, and one that probably offered an evolutionary advantage in fact, is that it allows us to understand each other as we empathize. And in turn, through that understanding we develop closer bonds with each other.

In evolution by natural selection, traits were selected if they improved the likelihood of survival. For instance, genes that produced muscles that could make a person fast and strong would confer an advantage over genes that produced weak and slow-moving muscles, especially when faced with a dangerous animal. So genes for strength and speed would be 'selected' by nature, meaning that within a few generations the only survivors would be those with fast and strong muscles.

Similarly, genes that promoted emotional contagion were selected because they encouraged strong bonds of kin and friendship that lent an advantage in the survival stakes. In past eras, our ancestors needed to band together to survive. They had to co-operate with one another and share resources. Strong bonds were an obvious requirement for this.

Today, a lot of our daily communication with each other relies on the transmission of emotion. We tend to think that it is only our words that matter. But have you ever sent an email that was misinterpreted because the recipient only saw the words, not the sentiment you wrote it with? If you were face to face, they might have seen your smile or unconsciously picked up on a subtle facial or bodily cue that would have let them know the real meaning in what you were saying.

Tapping into the same emotions as someone enables us to understand them far more clearly. This is why people with autism spectrum disorders have difficulty understanding people, because they don't absorb the emotions of others as efficiently.

## WOMEN TRANSMIT BETTER THAN MEN
On the whole, women are better transmitters of emotion than men are, although there are always exceptions.

In a 1974 study, volunteers viewed 25 different pictures that had been chosen to arouse emotion, like happy children, severe burns, facial injuries, scenic landscapes, nudity, art and unusual photographic effects. Expressivity was taken as a measure of transmission power.

The volunteers looked at each photograph for 10 seconds and then described their emotional reactions to it. There were hidden video cameras in the room which captured their facial expressions as they did so. The scientists also recorded the volunteers' autonomic nervous system (ANS) responses (heart rate and skin conductance).

The results showed that the powerful emotional transmitters tended to be women. They had the most expressive faces and a rich emotional language. Their ANS responses to the photographs, however, were not generally strong. As we express ourselves we don't build up emotion on the inside. Better out than in, as they say.

The weaker senders were generally male. Their facial expressions didn't show much emotion, although this didn't mean that they didn't feel emotion. On the contrary, their ANS responses were high, suggesting that they internalized their emotions, or were perhaps unwilling to admit that the photos had affected them. They might even have been unaware that they had been affected. Their language was also not as emotionally rich as the language that the women used.

Of course there were some men who were more expressive and some women who were less so. But in general, the women showed more facial movement than the men and gave a more personal verbal report of their emotions than the men did. They typically expressed their emotions, whereas the men tended to internalize theirs. Therefore there was a greater chance that their emotions would have been contagious.[5]

From one perspective, emotions want to be expressed, just as a flower wants to grow. When we don't express them, stress builds on the inside and our ANS response increases.

In another study, volunteers were shown 40 takes from movies that showed close-ups of actors displaying joy, sadness, fear and anger.[6] Twenty clips featured women and 20 featured men. Again, the results showed that the women were slightly better than the men at communicating emotion via their facial expressions. On the whole, there was little difference in the expression of joy, but the actresses seemed to be better at expressing fear and sadness and the actors better at expressing anger. Although Elizabeth is an actress and she seems to be able to get in touch with her anger fairly easily! (I hope she doesn't read that last sentence.)

A large number of studies have now confirmed that women are generally better transmitters of emotion than men. One meta-analysis examined 49 studies that looked at the differences between women and men in expressiveness and communication ability. The analysis clearly showed that women were more open and expressive than men.[7]

This will come as no surprise to most women, but it has now been scientifically proven that women generally smile more, laugh more, make more eye contact, are more tactile, move their body more and are generally freer in talking about their emotions than men.[8]

Fans of the sitcom *Friends* will remember the scene after Ross and Rachel's first kiss. Monica and Phoebe asked Rachel to describe the kiss, and gushed as Rachel described how Ross stroked her hair and tenderly kissed her. Ross, on the other hand, told Joey and Chandler about the kiss while the three of them were sitting eating pizza. All that happened was that Joey stopped eating for long enough to ask whether tongues had been used. Then they all carried on eating without further comment.

The difference in emotional expression starts early. In one study, it was found that infant girls expressed twice as much joy as infant boys, but that infant boys expressed twice as much anger, fear and distress as infant girls.[9]

By the teenage years, boys tend to grunt and mumble more, whereas teenage girls articulate their feelings better. This has much to do with puberty and boys getting used to speaking with a much deeper voice, but it probably does affect their expressivity in adulthood.

\*\*\*\*\*

We are all walking transmitters, sending out our mood from moment to moment in what we say and how we say it, in our facial expression and how we move our body. When we're happy we can infect others with happiness and when we're sad we can pass that on too.

We might pretend that we are feeling one way, but our face may betray us. Happy words can be masked with sadness in the eyes. But sad words can be wiped out by a smile.

> 'The typewriting machine, when played with expression, is not more annoying than the piano when played by a sister or near relation.'[10]
>
> Oscar Wilde

With knowledge of emotional contagion comes responsibility. We must take responsibility for what we transmit, just as we must be responsible for what we say and how we say it.

# SOAKING UP EMOTIONS

> 'Be careful [in] the environment you choose for it will shape you; be careful [in] the friends you choose for you will become like them.'
>
> W. Clement Stone

We are all susceptible to catching the emotions of others. But some of us are more susceptible than others.

In one way it's not such a good thing, especially if the people around us are sad, angry or anxious. The last thing we want is to pick up sadness, anger or anxiety. But in another way, picking up on these negative emotions helps us understand and sympathize with the people experiencing them and thus form strong bonds with them.

Most people would agree that being susceptible to emotional contagion is indisputably a good thing, however, if those around us are happy, positive, upbeat, confident or friendly. We like it when these things rub off on us. It takes little conscious effort to feel good among happy people. It's like a warm breeze on our face.

Because many emotions are conveyed through facial expressions, people who are good at reading expressions are also quite susceptible to picking up the emotions. Similarly, people who show empathy and feel compassion are also susceptible, as we learned earlier. We soak up emotions when we think of ourselves as connected to others, perhaps in a family, community or culture.

Unsurprisingly, people who are in love with each other are also quite susceptible to picking up each other's emotions. They focus admiringly on their partner and so are alert to their subtle emotional cues. Mothers also easily pick up on their baby's emotions. Also vulnerable to emotional contagion are therapists, teachers and carers. In general, whenever a person has a psychological investment in the well-being of another person, feels empathy for them and focuses their attention upon them, they are more susceptible to emotional contagion from them.[1]

Therapists can actually use emotional contagion to gain information about their clients' emotional state. In a 1992 paper published in the *Journal of Social and Clinical Psychology*, Christopher Hsee, Elaine Hatfield and Claude Chemtob write:

> *'Clinicians have identified two techniques for gaining information about clients' emotional states: (1) they can consciously try to assess clients' emotional states and/or (2) they can monitor their own emotional reactions during the therapeutic hour, hoping to "feel themselves into" their clients' emotion.'*[2]

Jung even felt it was a therapist's duty to share their clients' emotions so that they could better understand them.[3]

But if therapists are very sensitive to contagion, it can be difficult for them, especially if a client is depressed. Some therapists have been known to fall asleep when working with depressed clients. And of course this only compounds the depressed person's feelings of low self-worth!

In general, it takes effort not to pick up on people's emotions. When we are preoccupied with our own problems, however, this can swamp out the subtle signals we detect from others. Empathy is also dampened when we are low. When truly depressed, we are emotionally numb. When we are happy, on the other hand, we are generally more sensitive, because we aren't dwelling on our worries.

It is quite easy to consciously pick up on people's emotions. Stop projecting your own emotions, mimic the person subtly and just notice how you feel when you're with them. We do this unconsciously a lot and put it down to intuition, which of course it is. We have a feeling about a person, about how they are feeling. Emotional contagion forms part of the intuition equation, in a manner of speaking.

A 2009 study tested the accuracy of volunteers in identifying the emotional states of others, known as 'empathic accuracy'.[4] Volunteers who varied in emotional expressivity were videotaped while they discussed emotional events in their lives. Other volunteers viewed these videos in different ways. Some had the sound muted, some had only the sound and some watched the normal video.

The researchers found that being able to hear the words and vocal tones and see a person's expressions was important for empathic accuracy. Emotionally expressive volunteers were also easier to read.

Specifically, sound helped people better sense positive states. It seems we can still get loads of information from a person's face, but having their voice makes it much easier. I guess we take a lot from upwards inflections and other sounds that are typical of positive emotion.

Sound wasn't quite as necessary to understanding negative states. Seeing a scowl on a person's face kind of says it all!

The volunteers in the experiment were reading emotional states consciously. Of course, our brain does it unconsciously too – we just feel what others feel without even being aware of it. When we try to consciously evaluate the emotional state of another person, it depends on how well we translate the signals from our brain to our mind.

## 'I'M FINE'

Have you ever been with a friend who said they were fine but you sensed that something was up? Have you ever come away from being with a person who seemed OK feeling sad?

That we can read between the emotional lines was demonstrated experimentally by psychologists at the University of Hawaii in 1992. They asked subjects to view videotapes, supposedly of a Polish factory worker being interviewed at a high school reunion. The man was actually being asked to describe one of the happiest or one of the saddest moments of his life.

The psychologists created two different voiceovers using an actress faking a computer-like voice so that no emotional cues would be given. In one, the voiceover said that the man had been extremely happy at the time of the interview and in the other that he had been extremely sad.

The psychologists created four different video clips. In one, the voiceover said the man was happy at the time and he was indeed describing a happy event on the video (happy-happy). In another, it said that he was happy but he was actually describing a sad event (happy-sad). In the next, the voiceover said he was sad but he was actually happy (sad-happy) and in the last it said he was sad and he was indeed sad (sad-sad). The test subjects viewing the clips would therefore see facial expressions that might or might not correlate with what they were hearing on the voiceover.

Each volunteer watched one clip and was asked how they felt the man was feeling and how they felt themselves.

When the voiceover described the man as feeling happy and he really was happy, they rated him as happy and also felt happy themselves.

But when the voiceover described him as feeling happy but he was actually describing a sad event (happy-sad), they rated him as less happy than in the happy-happy video. And as they absorbed his real emotions from the video clip, they also felt less happy themselves. In fact they rated their own emotional state as slightly sad. Despite what the voiceover was saying, the man's emotions were contagious.

In the sad-sad clip, the volunteers rated the man as sad – specifically as −4.62 on the scale of happy (+) and sad (−) – and they felt sad themselves: −1.71.

But in the sad-happy condition (the voiceover saying the man was sad but he was actually happy), the volunteers still rated him as sad, though this was down to −3.18. They also rated their own state as slightly sad: −0.84.

This might sound as though the happiness wasn't contagious, but because the viewers didn't feel as sad as they had when watching the sad-sad video and hadn't rated the man as quite as sad either, his real happiness had filtered through somewhat. Happiness had been contagious in that it had reduced the impact of the voiceover. There had actually been a greater than 50 per cent improvement in the viewers' own emotions as they picked up on the man's true happiness from his facial expressions.[5]

What this tells us is that regardless of what people say to us, our own emotions can give us an intuitive sense of how they feel.

When an actor is playing a character in a film, TV programme or on stage, for instance, they might be saying dialogue but actually thinking of something else. We may pick up on this. When they *authentically* feel the emotions they are portraying, we feel it and are moved accordingly.

When actors are doing voiceover work, they smile because they know that the viewers can tell. Similarly, some customer service employees are taught to smile when they're on the phone. It can be contagious!

## WOMEN ARE EMOTIONAL SPONGES

Just as women are better emotional transmitters than men, they are also generally more susceptible to emotional contagion.

This was shown in a 1993 study of 884 people (535 men and 349 women) from a variety of ethnic backgrounds. Each of them was asked to complete the Emotional Contagion Scale questionnaire, which contained statements like 'Being with a happy person makes me feel light and cheerful' and 'When someone paces back and forth I feel nervous and anxious.' They had to rate each statement from 1 to 5, where 1 was 'not at all' and 5 was 'always'. A higher score on the questionnaire reflected a higher degree of emotional contagion.

The questionnaire tested the contagion of joy/happiness, love, fear, anger and sadness and general emotional contagion. Over all measures, the women were about 7 per cent more susceptible to catching the emotions. Specifically, they were 5 per cent more susceptible to catching joy than men and 5 per cent more susceptible to catching love. But they were much more susceptible to catching negative emotions: 13 per cent more susceptible to catching fear and sadness, although they were only 4 per cent more susceptible than men to catching anger.

On a very positive note, both women and men were found to be more susceptible to catching positive emotions than negative emotions.[6]

Part of the reason for women's higher susceptibility to all emotional contagion is that women (and girls) make eye contact faster and maintain it longer than men (and boys). Men (and boys) are more likely to avert their gaze. Women are also better at remembering faces and discerning emotions on faces.[7]

## INDEPENDENT OR INTERDEPENDENT?
How susceptible we are to picking up emotions has a lot to do with how we view the world and other people.

Some people view themselves as interconnected. Such a person would typically describe themselves in relation to others, for example 'I am a mother', or use words like 'we' and 'our' a lot.

A person who construes themselves as independent, on the other hand, would describe themselves more individually, typically saying things like, 'I am intelligent' and use 'I' a lot.

An interdependent view is more other-focused while an independent view is more self-focused. Most of us actually have a bit of both in us, but one will almost always be dominant.[8]

Culturally, the Western world is dominated by the independent view. Part of our culture is about striving for the best we can achieve. Personal independence is considered something to be proud of. We strive to express our individual strengths, often in competition with one another. We appreciate our differences and our uniqueness.

But in many Eastern cultures and some Latin American nations, and even the Native American tribes of the USA, there is a greater focus on our similarities than our differences. People from these cultures typically describe themselves in relation to each other – their families, friends, cultures, even their ancestors – and strive for a sense of harmony. It's not about standing out, but about togetherness.

There's a saying in the US that goes, 'The squeaky wheel gets the grease.' But an equivalent Japanese saying goes, 'The nail that stands out gets pounded down.'

These different construals impact many aspects of culture. In Western medicine, for example, there is a great focus on breaking things down into unrelated parts and treating those parts, whereas Eastern medicine takes a more holistic view, seeing the body and even the body and mind as a whole.

Of course, this is a broad generalization. There are many religious groups in the West who promote interdependence, like the Quakers, for instance. Many small towns and communities value interdependence too. And interdependence is also valued in the growing holistic movement.

It's worth noting that an interdependent view of self isn't about losing yourself in the identity of a group or culture or about your actions not being independent. It actually takes self-control, a mark of independence, to consider the impact of your actions on others and to maintain a sense of harmony with those around you.

To return to contagious emotions, seeing ourselves as connected to others, as interdependent, makes us more susceptible to their emotions. A friend is more likely to pass on their mood than someone you don't care for so much.

We can also get an indication of susceptibility by looking at how much a person mimics another. Those who mimic more, transmit and absorb emotions more, as we have already learned.

In a series of experiments, researchers from the University of Nijmegen and Ohio State University showed that whether we construe ourselves as interdependent or independent affects how much we mimic each other and therefore how susceptible we are to emotional contagion.[9]

In the experiments, Dutch volunteers were asked to read a total of 14 Polynesian sentences that had one word left blank in each. They had to then guess the Dutch translation of the word. One set of volunteers had to choose between 'I', 'me' and 'mine' and another set had to choose between 'he', 'him' and 'his'. In this way, the volunteers were primed with an independent self-construal – when they thought about 'I', 'me' and 'mine' – or an interdependent self-construal – when they thought about 'he', 'him' and 'his'.

An actor was also present in the room. The volunteers believed he was completing the task too, but he had been hired by the researchers. Approximately four times a minute he would either rub his face or shake his foot.

The volunteers who were primed with an interdependent view unconsciously mirrored the actor much more than those primed with an independent construal, and were completely unaware that they were doing it.

In a second experiment, participants were given 18 scrambled five-word sentences and instructed to make four-word grammatically correct sentences, for instance changing 'A bike fiercely rides he' to 'He rides a bike.' Those primed with an independent self-construal were primed with words like, 'unique', 'alone' and 'individual', and those primed with the interdependent self-construal were primed with words like 'together', 'group' and 'co-operate' and 'we', 'us' and 'our'.

This time, after completing the task, the volunteers were seated beside an experimenter who described a separate task to them while he played with his pen approximately five times a minute.

Those who were primed with the interdependent sense of self played with their pens much more than those in a control group, who in turn played with their pens more than those in the independent group.

In a third experiment, Japanese participants were compared with American participants. In each session a Japanese or American participant was seated opposite an actor, whom they thought was another participant, and shown a series of pictures which they were instructed to describe to each other. The actor rubbed his face or head/hair area constantly.

The results showed that the Japanese participants mirrored the face and head/hair rubbing behaviour much more than the Americans did. They also mimicked both Japanese and American actors equally.

Viewing ourselves as related to others brings us closer to them in our own mind. It reduces the emotional distance between us. As we draw closer to others in this sense, we unconsciously mimic their expressions and thus become more susceptible to emotional contagion.

Indeed, a 2008 study showed that viewing yourself as interdependent made you more likely to catch positive emotions from others.[10] In the study, led by researchers at the University of Houston, volunteers were asked to read a passage about a depressed or non-depressed person, who was described as having a low positive mood. Then their mood and sense of similarity to the person were assessed.

The volunteers who read the depressed passage reported lower mood than those reading the non-depressed one, indicating mood contagion. But specifically, the volunteers who rated themselves as similar to the person they read about, an indicator of interdependence, were found to be most susceptible to catching the low positive mood of the person they read about.

When we view ourselves as interdependent we look more to other people and less to ourselves. This immediately makes us more susceptible to emotional contagion. We see the people who share the space, community, country or planet with us as our extended family. We merge with them to some extent, even if it is in our own imagination. Emotions, attitudes and behaviour are then somewhat shared.

But what if it's not good for us to share?

# CHAPTER 7

# 'IT'S NOT MY STUFF': RESISTING EMOTIONAL CONTAGION

**'A work of art is one through which the consciousness of the artist is able to give its emotions to anyone who is prepared to receive them.'**

Muriel Rukeyser

What can we do to stop ourselves from soaking up people's negative emotions? (I'm assuming you're OK picking up positive ones.)

Here are a few ideas. They are by no means the result of a scientific study published in a journal, but are based on my own personal experience in the laboratory of my own life.[1] They may not work for everyone, but I hope they will educate, inspire and help.

As well as having plenty of our own stuff going on in our heads, the way to resist negative emotions is by becoming aware of emotional contagion. This awareness brings you back to yourself. You're no longer *feeling* the emotions but *observing* them; more to the point, you're observing how they're making their way to you. You're no longer lost in the situation.

You might like to bring your attention to your breathing. And notice that you are breathing. This brings your attention to yourself.

When you do this you dissociate yourself from the feelings and the situation provoking them. You become the watcher, of yourself. You might even mentally say, 'It's not my stuff.' This gives you control over the emotions and the situation in your own mind.

And it is mirrored in your brain. You activate the prefrontal cortex – the part of your brain that governs attention and willpower. Although this has not been described in studies on emotional contagion, which are more about transmitting and receiving than deflecting, we know this from studies on meditation. Becoming mindful of your breathing has been shown in several studies to activate this part of the brain.[2]

It also interrupts the neural circuit of the brain that is processing the emotion. Brain pathways tend to follow well-worn routes. Something happens, or you think about something, and you feel an emotion. At another time it happens again, or you think about the thing again, and you feel the emotion again. In time, the pathways get worn in, so to speak. When you stop and take a breath, you interrupt the 'journey' towards the emotion and therefore prevent the experience of the emotion at its end.

So, say your boss is angry and fumes at you. Afterwards you feel angry, anxious and hurt. Some of what you feel is of course your own. We all have our own 'stuff' that determines how we feel in certain situations. But in this situation part of what you are feeling is your boss's anger, even though you're internalizing it as your own. Even the feelings of anxiety that you assume to be your own could be your boss's underlying anxiety that was carried to you by subtleties in their expression, eyes, body language and voice.

When you stop and breathe and consider emotional contagion, you start to move away from the anger, anxiety and hurt. As a naturally empathetic person, you might even find yourself feeling compassion as you realize you are feeling your boss's pain.

This might not always work, or free you completely from the negative emotions, but at the very least it will lessen their impact. Of course, like most things, it does take practice.

Another way to deflect negative emotion is actually derived from the 'advice' that some animals give us: we can shake it off, just as a dog shakes off water when it gets wet! This gives the body a sudden change in physiology that is inconsistent with the negative emotion.

We can also intentionally change our physiology in some way. This is a good thing to do if you feel that you're in a negative environment. The longer you are in the environment, the more you are likely to pick up on the vibes and start to feel the same way. So adopt the physiology of happiness, or confidence, or power. It isn't possible to feel sad, angry or anxious if your physiology is saying, 'happy', 'confident' or 'power'. Fake it 'til you make it, as they say, or at least until you can shake off the emotions that you've absorbed.

To see how it works, try to feel sad for a moment. You might have to conjure up a thought or memory of something sad to do so. Now, are you smiling or frowning? Are the sides of your mouth pointing up or down? Are your shoulders forward or drooped? Have you dropped your head? Are you looking down? Are your lungs fully expired? You will notice that your physiology reflects the sadness. Many people, actors especially, actually use their physiology like this to rapidly enter an emotional state.

Now take a deep breath and smile. Lift your head up and pull your shoulders back. Try to feel sad. Any luck? I think not. It's very hard to feel sad when your physiology is saying 'happy'. We need the physiology to feel the emotion.

So, when you are in a negative environment and you think you are picking up on negative emotions, change your physiology. And if you have to spend any length of time in a negative environment, get good at mastering your physiology. If you can keep it the way you want it to be, you'll start raising the mood of that environment. It might not happen overnight, but the longer you stick with your new physiology, the more the group mood will move towards the mood reflected by your physiology. Set it as a goal – a project! It will keep your mind positive by giving you something to focus upon.

It is easier to keep your focus when you set this as a goal, rather than trying to avoid catching the negative stuff. These are two completely different focuses. It's like dieting. It is much easier to stick to a diet if you focus on how good food makes you feel than if you focus on trying to stop eating the fatty or sugary stuff. So, when in a negative environment, focus on how good the change in physiology makes you feel rather than on avoiding other people's emotions. Choose a sense of power.

Of course, there are times when you might want to pick up on negative emotions to share a friend or a loved one's emotions and genuinely appreciate their pain. This will deepen your connection and place you in a better position to help if you can.

Sometimes a person in pain just needs to talk, to express their emotions. When you empathize with them, when you allow yourself to be consumed by their emotions, you allow them to get them out of their system. And with awareness of contagion, you can shake them off later. In some ways you act like a vacuum cleaner of toxic emotion whose bag can be emptied later.

As we saw earlier, Jung's view was that it was a therapist's duty to share their client's feelings so that they could truly understand them and be in a better position to help. But on the whole, deflection strategies are useful for therapists who feel they are prone to soaking up their clients' emotions. They can then simply experience contagion to the degree that they wish in order to facilitate the empathy that is required. The key is awareness of what's going on.

For anyone who wants to gain emotional mastery, the first step is noticing how you are feeling and how that is showing up in your body.

So, practise becoming aware of your emotions. Catch yourself several times a day and notice how you are feeling in that instant. Notice how your body feels. Do you have tension in your face or mouth? Are they relaxed? How do your shoulders and neck feel? Relaxed or tense? What about your chest area? Are you feeling positive or negative, happy, determined, angry, sad or anxious?

If you are feeling a negative emotion, is it because of how you genuinely feel about your life, or have you recently been in a negative environment? Could you have been picking up someone else's emotions? Could you be doing it now?

You might have picked up an emotion and then tagged it to something in your own life. This is natural. The mind seeks to identify emotions with people and situations, and very often comes up with ones from the past. So, a negative feeling might conjure up all kinds of negative emotional memories from the past. It is easy to assume that the memories have just arisen by themselves, but it may be that the contagious emotion has triggered a memory that fits with that emotion.

So, ask yourself if the feelings first arose while you were in a negative environment.

If so, ask yourself whose emotions you are feeling. Trust your intuition here. You might suddenly get a picture of the person in your mind or get a feeling.

Of course, there are many times when an emotion is entirely your own, a product of your thinking or of something that has happened or is happening now. But it's good to be aware.

If you *have* picked up on someone else's stuff, recognize it as such. It's just a collateral feeling that you have been infected with. You don't need to keep it. Change your physiology or shake it off.

If you have absorbed anxiety from another person, it can be replaced by compassion or kindness towards yourself or that person.

If you feel another person is sad, anxious or depressed, you might wish to help. Send a text or card, or make a phone call, saying something kind, positive or uplifting about them. Make an attempt to raise their spirits.

This actually happened to me recently. I was feeling anxious and it was obvious that I was picking it up from a friend I'd been with a short time before. So I made a phone call, pretending to tell them something I'd forgotten to say, and made a point of paying them a compliment to raise their spirits. It really worked. My friend seemed much happier and I felt really good afterwards.

## BOTOX – A CHEMICAL ANTIDOTE TO EMOTIONAL CONTAGION?

We understand a person's emotional language by using some of the same circuits of the brain. The areas that govern facial expression play an important role in this.

Botox (botulinum toxin) can be used to paralyse the *corrugator supercilli* muscle (the frown muscle) to generate a smooth forehead. However, much of the transmitting and receiving of emotion requires some movement of the facial muscles. A person with total paralysis of the nerves of facial expression is unable to transmit any non-verbal facial cues whatsoever.[3]

So, when people get botox injections it can reduce their ability to transmit or soak up emotions. And because of this, a person injected with botox is not as good at really understanding people as the rest of us, because we unconsciously rely so much on facial mimicry for understanding.

This was shown in a 2010 study where 40 female volunteers read a sentence describing either an angry or sad or pleasant situation and then pressed a button as soon as they felt they understood it.

They then had botox injected to temporarily paralyse the *corrugator supercilli* muscle and read more sentences.

Compared with their responses before they had the injections, the volunteers took significantly longer to understand a sentence describing an angry situation after injection and a little longer to understand a sentence describing a sad one, but there was no difference in the length of time it took to understand a sentence describing a pleasant situation. This was because the botox didn't paralyse the facial muscles required to smile![4]

In a 2009 study, scientists at the Technical University of Munich tested the impact of botox on one of the areas of the brain used in the processing and generation of angry facial expressions (the amygdala). Twenty-eight women were asked to imitate an angry face and amygdala activity was found to be significantly reduced after the injection of botox into their frown muscles.[5]

An interesting side-effect of the use of botox to paralyse frown muscles therefore is that it might actually make us happier by reducing our ability to feel angry or sad.

Botox also affects our ability to generate a true smile, which uses the *orbicularis oculi* muscle that gives us the creases at the sides of our eyes that look like crow's feet. However, a 2008 report by scientists at the Department of Dermatology of Northwestern University hypothesized that it reduced negative facial expressions more than it reduced positive ones, creating a net positive effect on happiness by reducing the experiencing of negative emotions.[6]

I'm not sure if anyone has genuinely considered it, but there might be some mileage in using botox as a treatment for sadness or mild depression. By preventing frowning, it might make people feel happier. Similarly, a person having to exist in a toxic negative emotional environment might benefit from botox because their inability to mimic negative facial expressions would prevent them from absorbing the negative emotions of others.

*****

Resisting emotional contagion is a good thing if we are resisting negative emotion.

The key to resistance is *awareness* of emotional contagion. Then we are able to use changes in facial expression – perhaps a smile or two – and body language to establish our own emotions.

With control over our own facial expressions and no more unconscious mirroring going on, we feel how we want to feel and are not at the mercy of people who project strong negative emotion.

And with a little change in how we express ourselves, we can project our own emotions instead of being on the receiving end of those of others.

If we're projecting positive emotions in the midst of conflict, we might just move it towards peace.

# CHAPTER 8

# CONTAGIOUS DEPRESSION

'We allow our ignorance to prevail upon us and make us think we can survive alone – alone in patches, alone in groups, alone in races, even alone in genders.'

Maya Angelou

Depression can be contagious, as we've already learned. And it is far more prevalent than we might think. It is believed that by 2020 it could be the second most debilitating condition in the world, second only to heart disease.[1]

In fact, a study found that people born after 1945 were ten times more likely to suffer depression than those born before 1945.[2]

There are many different causes of depression. Some people are more at risk due to genetic factors, so that when stressful conditions arise in their lives they might get depressed, whereas other people might bounce back quickly from the same situation.

A person's social circumstances are also known to influence their risk of depression. People who are under heavy financial strain are more at risk. Being abused or bullied has a bearing on the risk factor, as do disruption in family life and stressful life events.

Giving birth and experiencing adverse career changes can also trigger depression. But it seems that it is also contagious. I think that just about everyone can relate to feeling low after spending time with someone who is depressed. It can even be contagious down the phone line.

In a 1976 study, volunteers were asked to phone a woman who was either depressed or not depressed and chat with her for 20 minutes. The scientists wanted to see if they would catch her depression. And they did. Those who chatted with a depressed woman became more depressed, anxious and hostile after the phone call than before. They had caught the woman's depression down the phone line.[3]

A 1985 study showed that depression could be passed between college roommates. On starting at Florida State University each new student completed the Beck Depression Inventory and was assigned a roommate. They completed the inventory again periodically over a three-month period and the results showed that students who had not been depressed when starting university but were now living with a mildly depressed roommate had become more depressed.[4]

Depression is also contagious within romantic relationships. A 2004 study led by scientists from Albert Einstein College of Medicine in New York and using a sample of 5,035 people from the Health and Retirement Survey (data from 1992 and 1994) found that having a depressed spouse was associated with significantly higher symptoms of depression at the follow-up test point.[5]

A 2006 study found a similar thing. Using data from a sample of 3,808 mixed-sex couples in marriages and relationships from the Household, Income and Labour Dynamics in Australia Survey (HILDA), scientists from the Australian National University in Canberra found concordance in the mental health of spouses.

They also found that similarity in the spouses increased in the first five years of a relationship, which ruled out 'like marrying like' as the main reason for both partners being depressed. One partner really had affected the other.[6]

And a 2007 paper that reviewed 103 individual concordance studies found overwhelming evidence of concordance within relationships in mental health, physical health and health behaviour.[7]

Many of the 103 studies didn't track changes in a person's depressive symptoms over a period of time, but taken together with the data presented so far, it seems likely that depression spread from one spouse to the other.

A 2010 study did, however, track changes over time. It involved 296 heterosexual couples and was led by researchers from Vanderbelt University and the University of Notre Dame. They found that a husband with depressive symptoms was associated with higher levels of depressive symptoms in his wife over time, and vice versa. In other words, if a husband was depressed it could actually cause depression in his wife over a period of time.[8]

Depression can be so contagious that entire families can become depressed together. It travels like a wave from parent to child, and when that child becomes a young adult they can pass it on to, say, a college roommate, and who knows where it goes after that? Just like a bug, depression can jump from one person to the next.

The best evidence to date for the contagiousness of depression comes from a study led by James Fowler, Professor of Medical Genetics at the University of California, San Diego, and Nicholas Christakis, physician and Professor of Medical Sociology at Harvard University, and was published in 2010.[9]

Fowler and Christakis studied the changes in mood of an entire interconnected social network over a period of time. The network was of the participants in the Framingham Heart Study, a long-term study initially of 5,124 people from the town of Framingham in Massachusetts, which was later expanded to include the children of the original participants, and then their children, totalling over 12,000 people.

The project began in 1948 and was designed to identify risk factors associated with cardiovascular disease. Much of what we know today about the links between diet, exercise, smoking, alcohol habits and cardiovascular disease originated from this study.[10]

Fowler and Christakis were able to reconstruct the social network of the original participants because staff on the Framingham Heart Study kept meticulously detailed handwritten records of each person's friends, family members, neighbours and co-workers as a way of keeping track of people throughout the course of the study. If anyone moved away, at least someone would know where to find them. The data also provided valuable information on people's lifestyle and mental health that could be used to track how depression spread.

One of the first things that Fowler and Christakis noticed when they analysed the data and reconstructed the social network using computer visual software was that depression appeared in clusters. Whole groups of people seemed to be depressed together.

Their statistical analysis of the data quickly ruled out the possibility that specific events were causing depression to happen to groups of people simultaneously or that depressed people were simply befriending each other. Depression really did spread from person to person.

For instance, the data revealed that if a friend of yours was depressed, it increased the likelihood of you being depressed by 93 per cent. And if it was a close friend, your likelihood increased by a staggering 359 per cent. But if someone considered you to be a friend and you didn't consider them a friend (a one-sided friendship), depression was not contagious from that person to you.

This fits with the other results that we have seen showing that emotions are more contagious if you like a person or if you feel a sense of connection with them. When someone isn't really your friend you don't empathize with them as much, or share their emotions. So the likelihood of them passing depression to you is non-existent.

And just as with emotional contagion, depression is also transmitted more efficiently by women than by men. Fowler and Christakis found that if a female friend was depressed it increased the probability that a person was also depressed by 142 per cent. Yet remarkably, when a male friend was depressed there was no increase in the probability of depression.

This makes sense when you consider that, as a broad generalization, women express emotions more than men, so they are more likely to show that they are depressed.

Both women and men were found to be susceptible to *catching* depression. It was just that women were better at passing it on than men.

Mirroring some of the research reported at the beginning of this chapter, spouses were also shown to pass depressive feelings on to each other, but the effect was relatively small in comparison to the transmission between friends.

It might be that with spouses, the 'like chooses like' factor, where we choose a person who is like us, is more widespread than with friendships. So people with a tendency for depression might marry people who also have that tendency. The likelihood of transmission is still there, but people in general are more likely to catch depression from their friends.

## YOUR POSITION IN A SOCIAL CIRCLE

The data also showed that the more friends and social contacts a person had, the less likely they were to become depressed. Given the likelihood of catching depression from friends, this might seem contradictory, but, just as biodiversity is related to the health of an ecosystem, so mental health (in a sense, the emotional ecosystem) is related to the number of personal connections.

The study found that being central to the network of friends, family and social ties, or even a section of it, was associated with much lower rates of depression. Being on the outskirts, on the other hand, i.e. having few contacts, was associated with higher rates of depression. As the authors wrote, '...depression depends upon how connected individuals are and where they are located within social networks.'[11]

They actually calculated that each social connection a person had reduced their depression score by 0.3 points (the scale ranges from 0 to 60, where 16 is defined as depressed).[12] Each non-depressed friend also reduced the risk of depression in the future.

Astonishingly, whether a person is depressed or not depends in part – at least as much as the influence of their genes – on how their friends are feeling!

The individual analysis points in the study were four years apart and found that the people who were depressed were, on average, likely to lose 6 per cent of their friends in this time compared with the people who showed no signs of depression.

And the impact of depressed people in the study was found to be six times greater than that of non-depressed people. As Fowler and Christakis noted, ' the feeling of depression seems to spread more easily than its absence.'[13]

It's interesting to consider that we are not as isolated as we think. How we feel is not only influenced by those we are immediately connected to but by the structure of the entire network that we are embedded in. It's like the actual structure of a forest affecting availability of food for a tiny insect, even though the insect only explores its local environment and obtains its food from there. We have no idea of the many influences that impact us every day, all helping to shape how we feel. We live in a much larger sphere of connectedness than any of us imagines.

## THREE DEGREES OF SEPARATION

Have you ever heard the term 'six degrees of separation'? It's the idea that every person is connected to every other person on Earth by no more than six connections. In other words, you know someone (1) who knows someone (2) who knows someone (3) who knows someone (4) who knows someone (5) who is friends with HH the Dalai Lama (6), or the Pope, or the King of Norway, the President of the United States, Brad Pitt or even Kevin Bacon.

The data from the Framingham Heart Study showed, astonishingly, that depression wasn't just contagious to friends, but travelled outwards by three degrees of separation, i.e. depression in one person not only affected their friends, but their friends' friends and their friends' friends' friends – people they didn't even know.

A person was 93 per cent likelier to be depressed if they had a friend who was depressed. But if they had a friend who had a friend who was depressed, a person at two degrees of separation whom they might not even have known, it increased their likelihood of depression by 43 per cent. And people at three degrees of separation still increased the likelihood of depression by 37 per cent.

Some researchers have suggested that the figures quoted in the study are artificially high and that with re-analysis they will be found to be lower. But even if they are, the effect is still there. The strength of the contagion may turn out to be lower or it may not, but depression is most definitely contagious.

One implication is that it might be beneficial for the health of an entire network to help depressed people who are socially isolated, because those with the fewest ties were found to have the highest depression scores. Because we are so interconnected, helping an isolated person will have a knock-on effect on many other people in the network who have neither met the person nor are ever likely to meet them.

This is what the data analysis clearly showed: the depression scores of even the most socially isolated people were correlated with the future depression scores of people who were more connected.

Think of it this way: say I have two friends, but through depression I gradually drift apart from one of them, Alistair. I now only have one tie. You might think that only affects me, but Alistair is now down one social tie too, which has a net effect on his mental health. And furthermore, the study showed that it's not just how many connections we have that affects our mental health but how connected our friends are. So the mental health of the people connected to Alistair is actually related to not only the number of connections they personally have, but also to the number of connections Alistair has.

So if I were depressed and socially isolated, I would actually affect the mental health of people embedded much more deeply in the social network. They may appear at first to be insulated by several friends and social connections, but their mental health is, without doubt, related to mine.

We cannot escape the fact that we live in an interconnected, holistic world. No one is isolated. Everyone matters. The weakest in society must be cared for, otherwise society itself will suffer.

Or, in the words of Martin Luther King Jr:

> 'In the final analysis, the rich must not ignore the poor because both rich and poor are tied in a single garment of destiny. All life is interrelated, and all men are interdependent. The agony of the poor diminishes the rich, and the salvation of the poor enlarges the rich. We are inevitably our brother's keepers because of the interrelated structure of reality.'[14]

## CONTAGIOUS LONELINESS

> 'Loneliness spreads across time… It travels through people. Instead of a germ, it's transmitted through our behaviours.'[15]
>
> John Cacioppo

Fowler and Christakis, together with John Cacioppo, who is director of the University of Chicago Center for Cognitive and Social Neuroscience, also used the Framingham Heart Study records to track the spread of loneliness. Just like depression, to which it is related, this was also shown to be contagious.

Lonely people tended to become lonelier. Just as with depression, they tended to shed some of their friends and move to the outside of social networks. But they still managed to infect some of their social network with loneliness on the way. Then these new lonely individuals moved towards the outside too, again infecting other contacts first.

You can see how it works. Say you have three friends and one of them for whatever reason stops calling and you gradually drift apart. Now you're down to two friends. The reality of that hits you and you start to feel insecure and lonely. This is a self-fulfilling prophecy because you then start to behave as if you're lonely – you become shy and anxious and think there's something wrong with you – and so you drift away from your two remaining friends, causing one or more of them to start to feel lonely.

## ANOTHER THREE DEGREES

It might come as no surprise to learn that, just as with depression, loneliness also spreads out to three degrees of separation. Having a friend who is lonely makes you 40–65 per cent more likely to be lonely. At two degrees of separation, a friend of a friend who is lonely makes you 14–36 per cent more likely to be lonely; at three degrees of separation, a friend of a friend of a friend who is lonely increases your odds of loneliness by 6–26 per cent. The effect peters out at four degrees.[16]

\*\*\*\*\*

We are all deeply and irrevocably interconnected. The sooner we really understand this, the quicker we can take real steps towards a better world. We must look out for everyone. One depressed or lonely person affects all of us. As Fowler and Christakis wrote, 'People are connected, and so their mental health is connected.'[17]

# CHAPTER 9

# FROM NON-CONTAGIOUS TO CONTAGIOUS

**'I've been on a diet for two weeks
and all I've lost is two weeks.'**
Totie Fields

There is little doubt that there is currently an obesity epidemic. Levels of obesity have risen dramatically over the past 20 years. According to the World Health Organization, there are currently 1.6 billion overweight adults and more than 400 million of them are obese. And it further predicts that there will be 2.3 billion overweight adults by 2015, of whom 700 million will be obese.[1]

Childhood obesity is also rife. Again according to the World Health Organization, over 42 million children under the age of five were overweight by 2010.[2]

There is no doubt of the epidemic, but what we greatly under-estimate is the effect obesity has on our health. Among other diseases, it increases the risk of heart disease and diabetes.

Diet and lifestyle factors are mostly blamed for the rise. Yet one factor in the spread that hasn't been considered is how much we affect each other – or at least it hadn't been considered until Christakis and Fowler published a landmark study in 2007, offering a fresh view on the epidemic. This exciting research shows that your chances of putting on weight increase if some of your friends put on weight.[3] Obesity is contagious.

Once again using data from the Framingham Heart Study, the researchers found that, just like depression, obesity was present in clusters and also spread from person to person through social networks, just like a virus or bacteria jumps from one person to the next.

And it spread efficiently. In 1948, less than 10 per cent of Framingham residents were obese. This had risen to 18 per cent by 1985, and by early in the twenty-first century, approximately 40 per cent of the population were obese.[4]

And, again as with depression, our friends play a considerable role in our weight and the influence extends out to three degrees of separation.

## OBESITY AND FRIENDSHIP

The pattern for the type of friendship was the same with obesity as it was with the depression analyses of the data. Having an obese friend increased a person's risk of obesity by 57 per cent, but in close friendships the risk of becoming obese by the next time measurement increased by a staggering 171 per cent. And again, people were only affected by those they felt close to.

Obesity was more contagious within the sexes than between them. The risk increased by 71 per cent if a same-sex friend became obese (averaged over all types of friends and social contacts), but there was no seeming transmission from male to female or female to male friends.

Like depression, obesity is contagious throughout social networks, but the mode of transmission is different. Depression involves mirror neurons and so the transfer of emotions; obesity, on the other hand, travels by altering thoughts. It alters social perceptions. We might attach a social stigma to obesity, but then a friend gains weight and we see that they are just as happy as they were before. So we re-evaluate our perception of obesity, shifting it in a positive direction. Now that we have let our social barrier down, we become more susceptible to catching it.

Obesity is a virus, but not a physical one. It is a virus of the mind.

We're more likely to shift our perspective if we are the same sex as the obese person because the new perspective is more relevant to us. A woman might become OK with weight gain if she saw that her newly obese best friend was still happy, still herself, could still dress nicely and look attractive and could do all the things they had always done together. But if her best friend was a man, it wouldn't have the same effect upon her because men and women often do different things, and they dress differently.

The contagion is actually higher between male friends than between female friends. If one male friend became obese, it raised the chance of the other becoming obese by 100 per cent, but it was only 38 per cent between females. Maybe this is because women are more conscious of their weight than men.

The effect is reversed within families. With brothers, if one became obese the chances of another following was increased by 44 per cent. But the effect was higher with sisters, at 67 per cent. But again, there was no apparent transmission across the sexes from brother to sister or sister to brother.

The only exception, where obesity *was* contagious across the sexes, was within marriages. Husbands becoming obese increased the wives' risk by 44 per cent and wives becoming obese increased the husbands' risk by 37 per cent. This is more likely to be due to them adopting similar dietary habits than changing perspective. But it shows that obesity can jump the sex barrier.

## YOUR SISTER'S HAIRDRESSER'S BEST FRIEND CAN MAKE YOU FAT

Unlike depression, which requires people to see each other to activate mirror neurons, the geographical distance between friends has little bearing on the contagiousness of obesity.

In the study, the contagiousness of obesity was much the same regardless of whether the person lived one mile or ten miles away. It seems that social perceptions can change down the phone line or with very little contact.

But social distance matters. The average risk of obesity if a social contact became obese was 45 per cent. But if a friend of a friend became obese, someone at two degrees of separation, it increased a person's risk of becoming obese by 20 per cent. Someone three degrees removed still increased the obesity risk by 10 per cent.

So, imagine Carrie is your sister and she keeps a monthly appointment with her hairdresser, Charlotte, whom she also considers a friend. Charlotte also has a best friend called Samantha, whom you have never met.

Now if Samantha, for any one of a number of reasons, gains a lot of weight, then according to these results there is a fairly high chance (171 per cent increased risk) that Charlotte will also gain a similar amount of weight (to be classified as obese) over the next six months. And because she is having regular hairdressing appointments with Charlotte, as well as friendly conversations, there is also a fairly high risk that Carrie will gain weight. And Carrie being your sister that means that there is a good chance that you will gain weight too.

Carrie is at one degree of separation from you, Charlotte at two degrees and Samantha at three degrees. On average, summing up all types of social contacts, you have at least a 10 per cent increased risk of becoming obese if Samantha becomes obese, even if you've never actually met her.

I guess you could truthfully say that your sister's hairdresser's best friend can make you fat!

## 'I CONCUR'

We affect our romantic partners in many ways. We influence their weight. But we also influence their smoking and drinking, whether they exercise or not and how much they exercise. We even influence the type of food they eat. Our habits spread to them and theirs to us. In many ways this can be a good thing, but it can also be dangerous.

We can increase a spouse's risk of developing heart disease, for instance. Increasing their obesity risk has a direct bearing on their heart disease risk, for a start.

A 2000 study of 177 men with coronary heart disease and their spouses found an increased risk of coronary heart disease in the spouses. The study found significant concordance in body mass index, history of smoking, current smoking status, how much exercise the couples took and the amount of fat and fibre in their diet, all of which are known to be risk factors for coronary heart disease.[5]

Of course, sceptics might argue that 'like attracts like'. People with similar habits, and weight as the case may be, form relationships with one another. But it's not a case of either/or, *but* that obesity is transmitted *and* we marry people like us.

In light of the evidence presented so far, I am sure you will agree that contagiousness of attitudes and habits plays a large role in the transmission of obesity within romantic relationships.

A 2010 study found a concordance in a number of risk factors for metabolic syndrome in families.[6] The scientists used a sample of 174 married couples aged between 28 and 63, where one person within the marriage had premature coronary heart disease (which is onset before the age of 55). They measured alcohol consumption, smoking, education level, body mass index (BMI), waist circumference (WC), heart rate, blood pressure (BP), low- and high-density lipoprotein cholesterol, triglycerides (TG), apoproteins I and B, lipoprotein A, blood glucose, insulin, homoeostasis model assessment-insulin resistance (HOMA IR), fibrinogen and activity of plasminogen inhibitor type 1. They found concordance in every single one of the measures!

The study did not track the changes over time to investigate if one spouse affected the behaviour of the other. That was not its purpose. And of course there will be many instances in large samples of people where people do enter into relationships with someone who is similar to them, and therefore the risk factors will be pretty similar at the start of the relationship. And there will also be examples where something influences both of them at the same time, like TV advertising for instance.

But taken together with other network research, it seems almost certain that hidden within these results lies the effects of contagion, just as hidden in a landscape painting are patterns of colour that you would not see unless you looked closely. The main tones obscure deeper patterns.

## CONTAGIOUS WEIGHT LOSS

What about it going the other way? Could weight loss be contagious? So far, a large network hasn't been studied for this, but other evidence does suggest that it is in fact the case.

In a 2007 study, scientists from the University of Connecticut enrolled 357 overweight patients with type 2 diabetes onto a weight loss programme that was part of the Look AHEAD (Action for Health in Diabetes) programme. Each patient and their spouse was weighed at the start of the programme and then again after 12 months.

As was the purpose of the programme, the diabetes patients lost weight, but the study also showed what the authors referred to as a 'ripple effect'. The spouses of each of the diabetes patients also lost weight – an average of 5lb over the course of the study.

The scientists proposed that social networks could be used to promote the spread of weight loss.[7]

Healthy behaviour is contagious too.

## CONTAGIOUS HEART DISEASE

The Christakis and Fowler research clearly shows that friends and husbands and wives can influence the likelihood of each other becoming obese. And, as already noted, obesity is a risk factor for heart disease.

In a very real sense then, heart disease is contagious – not as a bacteria or a virus that infects our biology, but as a consequence of contagious habits and attitudes. It is the mind that is infected with the seeds that grow into heart disease.

If a woman who has grown up on a healthy diet marries a man who has always had an unhealthy diet, they will affect each other. They will either meet somewhere in the middle or the husband will eat more healthily or the wife more unhealthily. If one partner becomes unhealthier as a consequence of the other's dietary habits then their risk of heart disease will have increased. This is common sense and I'm sure many readers have experiences in this arena.

Before I met Elizabeth my diet was OK, but it was not what a qualified nutritionist would call healthy. For instance, my average lunch was four white bread spam or cheese sandwiches (I rotated them each day). I also drank lots of soft drinks and rarely ate salad or vegetables.

Elizabeth enjoyed a much healthier diet than me. But my diet gradually improved when we got together, mainly because we would eat together and it would have been silly to prepare two different meals. I moved in Elizabeth's direction rather than Elizabeth moving in mine – so I guess you know who wears the trousers in our relationship!!

My diet changed radically in 2003, when I went to a lecture on nutrition. Without much effort I also lost 18 pounds in weight in seven weeks and felt much lighter in body and mind. And why did I attend that lecture? Because Elizabeth dragged me along!

Contrary to popular beliefs, heart disease is not mostly genetic. Genetics does have an influence, and a relatively small percentage of cases of heart disease are strongly genetic, but on the whole heart disease is mostly a product of lifestyle. A family history of heart disease makes it appear that a person might have heart disease genes, but also running in families are lifestyles, attitudes and emotions.

So, if dietary habits can be contagious then they can carry heart disease with them.

Looking at attitudes, it is now very clear that hostility and aggression are significant risk factors for heart disease, as much so as diet and exercise levels. Many studies have now shown that those who are most hostile and aggressive in how they treat people are at greater risk of heart disease than those who are gentler in how they relate with people.[8] And as we know, we can catch aggression from others. It is contagious.

If a child contracts aggression from a parent, or even from a group of friends, and does not make any changes in attitude as they grow into adulthood, then their risk of heart disease will have increased on account of the aggression that they were infected by.

Heart disease is not the only medical condition that can develop in this way. It is widely accepted, for instance, that many cases of cancer are due to lifestyle factors. Obesity is again a risk factor, for instance. It is these lifestyle factors that are contagious. So if we catch a form of unhealthy behaviour from a friend or family member then the cancer risk will spread.

Any classically non-contagious disease that is lifestyle-related can become contagious through contagious thinking.

# THE BENEFIT OF BEING CONNECTED

*'A healthy attitude is contagious but don't wait to catch it from others. Be a carrier.'[9]*

Tom Stoppard

Being connected to others increases our risk of disease through bacterial or viral transmission, emotional or behavioural contagion, or even mindset contagion. The more connected we are, the higher the risk.

But being connected is also good for our health. Studies show, for instance, that good relationships and multiple social ties not only reduce depression but are also good for the heart.[10] It is not totally clear whether it is being connected itself that provides the heart benefits or whether being connected allows for the contagiousness of good behaviour or whether it is a bit of both.

Being connected certainly provides a fertile environment for the transmission of positive emotions and behaviour. But it does seem that it is healthy in itself.

In 2010 researchers at Brigham Young University published a meta-analysis of 148 individual studies involving 308,849 people, of an average age of 63.9 years and from four different continents, that dealt with the impact of social relationships on mortality risk. The conclusion was startling: people who enjoyed strong social ties had a 50 per cent increased likelihood of survival over a period of 7.5 years compared with people with weak or no social ties.[11]

The strength of the effect is astonishing. It is comparable with, or better than, the impact of having a typical healthy lifestyle. Having strong social ties is as important to longevity as eating a healthy diet and exercising regularly. It is as influential as blood pressure, smoking habits, alcohol habits and obesity.

The people we're friends with, and the quality of our relationships, matter much more than we think.

Despite the evidence staring us in the face, building strong family and social ties is not really taken very seriously. But consider, as the authors of the study rightly point out, that it wasn't so long ago that researchers noted the very high mortality rates of children brought up in institutions. Lack of contact was a death sentence to some.

Indeed, found in the diary of a Spanish bishop in 1760 were the words, '*En la Casa de Niños Expósitos el nino se va poniendo triste y muchos de ellos mueren de tristeza.* [In la Casa de Niños Expósitos (Home to the Exposed), children can become so sad that many of them even die of sadness.]'[12]

In a 1951 article, child psychiatrist John Bowlby, who had compiled a report pointing out the mental and physical health of orphaned and institutionalized children, wrote of the disbelief and academic resistance to his work:

> '*Reception was mixed. Those with practical experience of the problem, notably social workers, psychologists, and psychiatrists dealing with children, were enthusiastic. Learning theorist psychologists were bitterly critical, pointing to the deficiencies of the data and the lack of theory to link alleged cause and effect.*'[13]

But these studies and writings eventually prompted substantial changes, and a great deal of research is now focused on the long-term health effects of institutionalization and the benefits of fostering and adoption. Among these is the Bucharest Early Intervention Project, which has shown that children who are adopted or fostered fare much better than those brought up in institutions. The brain develops much better and their physical bodies actually grow taller.[14]

UNICEF, in fact, notes that for every three months a child spends in an institution, it loses a full month of growth.[15] Being fostered or adopted at an early age is associated with 'massive catch-up'.

As a result of this type of research, mortality rates in institutions have dropped dramatically. I believe it is about time for a similar recognition of the importance of social relationships in adults. It is clear that having friends saves lives. Social isolation is harmful to our health. The longer we ignore the fact that we need to connect, the worse for all of us.

One of the best examples of the beneficial effects of connection is known as the 'Roseto effect'.[16] Roseto is a small town on the east coast of the United States of America. During a census in the 1960s it was discovered that the death rate for heart attack in the under 50s was almost non-existent. It was actually 1971 before the first person under the age of 45 died of a heart attack.

It turned out that what protected them was each other. There was a very high degree of social interconnectedness in Roseto. People were more connected than in other towns and cities in the United States. Many households, for example, had three or four generations of family living there. Regular social events would see most of the town turn out. Everyone knew everyone else.

Any new additions to the town would immediately 'catch' the seeming immunity to heart disease. Their diet might have been the same as in their previous town of residence, but what changed was their connectedness.

Romantic relationships provide particularly deep bonds. There is a wealth of evidence that marriage is good for our health and even helps us to live longer.

The first scientific research showing the health benefits of marriage was conducted in 1858 by British epidemiologist William Farr.

Using statistics from France, he examined the mortality rates of people who were married, unmarried and widowed. He found that married people lived longest and widowed died youngest.[17]

We now know that it's not the marriage itself that causes these effects, but the quality of relationship within the marriage that matters most. If a marriage is particularly stressful, it can increase the chances of heart disease. Good-quality relationships matter. They also improve the likelihood of contagion, but the relationships themselves matter irrespective of what is transmitted through them.

## OXYTOCIN: BIOLOGICAL-SOCIAL GLUE

There is now strong evidence that some of the health benefits of being connected might have a lot to do with the hormone oxytocin.[18]

We produce oxytocin when we connect with each other. We produce it when we hug, when we touch, when we're in love and even when we make love. Stroking a pet produces oxytocin, as does feeling connected to a spiritual deity. Even feeling inspired produces it. In all of these circumstances, it is the sense of connection that is common. When we connect, we produce oxytocin.

The reverse also applies: having lots of oxytocin also encourages us to form bonds with each other. In this way, oxytocin serves as a kind of biological, or social, glue that holds us in relationships. There are high levels of it in good-quality relationships.

Oxytocin, in fact, is believed to have played a substantial role in evolution and is one of the reasons why we are here today. It encouraged our ancient ancestors to stick together, to care for their young and to live together in small communities that offered greater protection against predators and the elements than living alone.

We can see the effects of these connections in simple studies that examine our ability to recognize facial expressions.

For instance, in a 2010 study 50 volunteers were either given oxytocin or a placebo as a nasal inhalation. Then they were shown a range of different faces, showing happiness, surprise, anger, disgust, fear or sadness, that were morphed with neutral faces in varying degrees from 10 per cent to 100 per cent intensity. So sometimes the expression was clear, but other times it was subtle. The researchers found that the volunteers who had received oxytocin were much better at identifying happy facial expressions.[19]

As well as enhancing our ability to recognize facial expressions, oxytocin helps us to interpret the emotions of other people. It improves co-operation and trust. It even makes us more generous. It improves empathy, and empathy is a key part of emotional contagion.

I propose that oxytocin plays a key biological role in emotional contagion, especially of positive moods, and may also play a role in the mirror neuron system.

I also propose that oxytocin is the biological glue that holds networks together and thus facilitates contagion of emotions, behaviour, attitudes and mindsets.

## IT'S WRITTEN IN YOUR EYES

It seems this is because, overall, oxytocin improves our ability to detect the emotional state of others, and part of the cue comes from the eye region of the face.

According to 2008 research at the University of New South Wales, oxytocin causes us to focus more attention on this region, a place where key emotional information is displayed. In the study, 52 male volunteers were shown 24 neutral faces after they had inhaled either oxytocin or a placebo. The researchers found that those who had received oxytocin focused their gaze much more on the eye region compared with those who had received a placebo.[20]

From the eye region we can obtain information about happiness or sadness from contractions of the *orbicularis oculi* muscle, which is associated with a genuine smile (which we'll come to later), or the *corrugator supercilli* muscle, which contracts to produce a frown.

A 2007 study examined our ability to work out the mental states of others from their facial expression – something researchers refer to as 'mind reading'. Using the Reading the Mind in the Eyes test (RMET), a test that involves looking only at the eye regions of faces, the study of 30 males found that oxytocin improved the ability to 'mind read'.[21]

The pupils may also play a role in emotional contagion. In a 2006 study, researchers at the Institute of Neurology and the University of London found that pupil size modulated perception of people's emotional expressions. The viewer's own pupil size adjusted to match that of the person in the photo they viewed.[22]

## THE CARDIOPROTECTIVE EFFECT

Oxytocin plays a key role in reducing risk of heart disease and I believe that it plays a central role in *why* good-quality relationships and connectedness are associated with better health of the heart.

We know that oxytocin lowers blood pressure, for instance. It produces nitric oxide in our arteries, causing vasodilation, or the expansion of our blood vessels. When this happens the heart doesn't need to work so hard to pump blood and oxygen through the body, so blood pressure is reduced. Oxytocin is therefore a cardioprotective hormone.

Studies have shown that it also reduces the levels of free radicals and inflammation throughout the body. Studies on stressed blood vessel cells and immune cells showed that oxytocin reduced levels of free radicals by up to 48 per cent and inflammation by up to 57 per cent[23] – a staggering reduction, considering that all we have to do to produce oxytocin is to connect with each other.

It is my opinion that oxytocin, our biological-social glue, is what protected the residents of Roseto from heart disease. Free radicals and inflammation play a central role in heart disease, so by keeping levels low, oxytocin reduces the risk of heart disease and therefore promotes longevity.

## USING CONTAGION TO REDUCE DISEASE
We know that contagion can spread emotions and behaviour, but what about spreading healthy behaviour that might prevent or slow the spread of disease?

Scientists have been using network knowledge to try to slow the spread of HIV infections and getting excellent results.

Some studies have targeted leaders within drug-using HIV communities, because they are often the most connected and thereby able to transmit information to more people. In one study, researchers identified 36 people whom drug users had nominated as leaders in the IDU (injecting drug users) community. These leaders were then given training in how to be 'opinion leaders' within their networks of drug users and sexual partners.

The study found that, compared to a control group, the opinion leaders used condoms significantly more often and always used bleach to clean their needles before use. But, importantly, members of their networks also started using bleach to clean their needles and were also much less likely to share their needles. Remarkably, the study reported 2,165 individual HIV prevention actions throughout the networks.[24]

In a review of many of the network interventions, Dr Alan Neaigus, principal investigator at the Institute for AIDS Research at National Development and Research Institutes, Inc., in New York City, wrote:

*'HIV is transmitted, in large part, by risk behaviours that involve close contact between infectious and susceptible individuals. As a result, the transmission of HIV is structured by social relationships. These social relationships organize how susceptible and infectious individuals come into contact with one another, the pattern of HIV exposure and transmission, and, through social influence, the risk of protective behaviours in which they engage with each other.'*[25]

In other words, even though HIV is a biologically contagious disease that is transmitted through bodily fluids, that alone is not enough to make it contagious. People must come into contact with one another. It is our social connectedness that provides the mental and emotional medium that facilitates the transmission.

And so, rather than focusing all efforts on tackling the virus at the biological level, there is much scope for working on the social environment within which it is transmitted. We don't need to prevent people connecting, of course. That is a biological necessity. But we can use that connectedness to transmit information that lessens the likelihood of HIV being transmitted and to transmit positive behaviour.

We can also use our connectedness to rid society of the stigma attached to the disease. As the late Princess Diana said, 'HIV does not make people dangerous to know, so you can shake their hands and give them a hug! Heaven knows they need it.'[26]

## NON-VERBAL COMMUNICATION AND HEALTH CARE

We know that as well as transmitting our intentions and emotions in our language, we also transmit them through our non-verbal behaviour. A frown transmits anxiety while a smile transmits happiness. Even having your back to someone transmits information – the idea that you don't care for them, for instance, or that you're not interested in them at that time. And what you transmit might stop there, or might be passed on to two degrees of separation or further.

Some studies have begun to investigate the consequences of such non-verbal transmission in the healthcare environment.

It has now been shown that the non-verbal communication between a patient and healthcare practitioner plays a considerable role in patient outcome. When a patient is satisfied with their doctor's communication, they are much more likely to stick with the course of their medication and have a better outcome.

For instance, in a 1988 study of diabetes patients where patients were encouraged to interact with their doctor and negotiate medical decisions more, they felt more satisfied with the session. After the intervention, the patients who had interacted more had a much healthier glycosated haemoglobin (HbA1) level than a control group.[27]

In a 2002 study, conducted jointly by researchers at Harvard University, Stanford University and the University of California at Riverside, physiotherapists were videotaped during sessions with clients to identify their non-verbal behaviour. Sections of the tape were then viewed by judges who rated the non-verbal communication of the therapists. The physical, mental and emotional functioning of the clients was measured at the start of the study, at discharge and again three months after discharge.

The researchers found that the therapists' non-verbal behaviour was linked with the patient outcome.

Where a therapist showed distancing behaviour, through not smiling and looking away from the client, there were short- and long-term decreases in the client's physical and mental functioning. This sort of non-verbal behaviour can convey to a client that their prognosis is not good. A therapist's lack of emotional warmth can therefore be transferred to a client and affect their ultimate outcome.

However, when the therapists showed facial expressions – smiling and even frowning – and also when they nodded – in other words, when they were connecting with their clients – this was associated with both short- and long-term improvements in the clients. It wasn't so much the facial expression that mattered, just that the therapist was bonding. Bonding increases emotional contagion and also a therapist's belief that a client will improve, and subtle gestures like these also give a client more faith that they will recover.

The researchers stated, 'It is now widely accepted within the medical profession that treatment regimen alone cannot fully account for patient outcome.'[28]

Doctors and therapists around the world are now being given education not just in *what* to do, but in *how* to do it.

In a 2009 meta-analysis of 127 similar published studies, researchers at Texas State University found that among patients of physicians who communicated poorly there was 19 per cent less adherence to the full treatment regimen than with patients of physicians who communicated well. Poor communication is a barrier to connectedness.

The researchers concluded:

> *'Training physicians in communication skills results in substantial and significant improvements in patient adherence such that with physician communication training, the odds of patient adherence are 1.62 times higher than when a physician receives no training.'*[29]

The effect on patient health, then, is considerable.

**\*\*\*\*\***

To sum up, through our connections we transmit emotions, behaviour, attitudes and mindsets to each other which may be healthy or unhealthy in the long term.

Diseases and other medical conditions that are not contagious in the classical sense of infection by a bacterium or virus *are* actually still contagious. They are transmitted by the mind and travel along the 'wires' of our emotional connections with one another.

In and of itself, however, being connected makes us both mentally and physically healthier, even to the point of lengthening our lifespan.

# CHAPTER 10

# CONTAGIOUS FEAR

**'Fear defeats more people than any other one thing in the world.'**
Ralph Waldo Emerson

How do you feel if you see someone showing fear?

In a 2007 study, researchers at Columbia University and New York University showed how fear can jump from one person's brain to another.

The study involved 11 people who lay inside an MRI scanner and watched a short video of a volunteer receiving electric shocks while carrying out a task. The scanner showed activation in the amygdala area of the volunteers' brains as they watched the person expressing fear.

Then, after a short break, they were told that they would now be taking part in the task themselves. This immediately produced fear in the volunteers.

When reviewing the scans, the researchers found that the amygdala was activated in both cases. The brain reacted in the same way regardless of whether the person was feeling fear themselves or just looking at someone else experiencing fear.

The researchers commented, 'Indirectly attained fears may be as powerful as fears originating from direct experiences.'[1]

In another study, participants viewed a still image of an actor reeling backwards on opening a door and being confronted by a robber. They could not see his face because it was blacked out; they could only see his bodily expression of fear. But the fear was still transmitted. The participants' brains reacted as if they themselves were being confronted by the robber.[2]

This makes sense from an evolutionary point of view. Our ancestors would have needed to know when those around them sensed danger. So our brains evolved to recognize bodily expressions of fear. Now, the 'fight or flight' response is stimulated by any fearful movement of the body.

It has also been hypothesized that fear, or at least danger contagion as bodily movement, is responsible for the sudden change in flight direction of a flock of birds when they are faced with danger.[3]

In a 1984 study, researchers at the University of Wisconsin near Madison showed that young monkeys became intensely afraid of snakes after watching their parents react with fear to a snake, or even a toy snake, for just a few minutes.[4]

Do you know anyone who reacts to something with the same fearful facial expressions, words or mannerisms as their parents do, or their grandparents?

In another experiment conducted at the University of Wisconsin near Madison, monkeys who were not related to the monkeys who were fearful of snakes but were acquainted with them caught a fear of snakes from them after only eight minutes of watching them behave fearfully in the presence of snakes. Then when these monkeys served as models for other unrelated monkeys, the new set of observers also caught the fear of snakes from them.[5]

Fear can ripple outwards like an infectious disease. As well as humans and monkeys, many different animals have shown susceptibility to fear contagion, including birds, rodents, cats and primates.[6]

Fear is contagious both through facial expressions and bodily movements, and of course through what we say to each other too. We may transmit particular fears, but also simply fear itself, which the person receiving it will then attach to something in their own experience.

The effects of fear go beyond the brain. Fear affects the nervous system, the immune system and the chemistry of the body. Research has shown various changes throughout the autonomic nervous system when we see someone look fearful.[7] The amygdala sends signals to the hypothalamus area, which manufactures chemical substances that can lead to actual body chemistry changes. It seems that some of these changes can even bring about symptoms of illness.

## MASS PSYCHOGENIC ILLNESS

*'Mass psychogenic illness is characterized by symptoms, occurring among a group of persons with shared beliefs regarding those symptoms.'[8]*

Timothy F. Jones, MD

Mass psychogenic illness (also known as mass sociogenic illness, MSI, or mass hysteria) works like the nocebo effect, which is the inverse of the placebo effect. Where placebo comes from the Latin, 'I shall please', nocebo comes from its opposite, 'I shall harm.' If a person takes a placebo, for instance, thinking it's a real drug, and is pessimistic about the benefits or expects to get worse, their own attitude, belief and expectations might bring on negative symptoms.[9]

Similarly, when a person smells something that has caused someone else to, say, faint, their own beliefs might bring on negative symptoms that are severe enough for them to require hospital treatment. This is how a mass psychogenic illness can start.

It is a much more common phenomenon than you might think. A large-scale epidemiological study published by researchers at King's College London in 2010 which examined a random sample of 280 chemical incidents found that 19 of them (7 per cent) were probable episodes of MSI.[10]

As fears have changed throughout history, the types of mass psychogenic illness have also changed to reflect the common fears of the times.[11] Before 1900, for instance, most reports are of agitated movement and personality, excitation, exuberance, loss of control and dancing. In the Middle Ages, some outbreaks involved people being seemingly possessed by spirits, which mirrored the popular fears of those times. There were also dancing manias where tens, hundreds and sometimes thousands of people danced uncontrollably, with arms flailing bizarrely, shouting, screaming and sometimes singing until they eventually collapsed out of exhaustion.

When we think of a plague we tend to think of something like the Black Death, but in Strasbourg, France, in July 1518, a woman known as Frau Troffea started dancing passionately in a narrow street. She danced continuously for four to six days before collapsing out of utter exhaustion. But her dance moves caught on. By the end of the week, 34 people were dancing uncontrollably. Within a month the 'dancing plague' had spread to around 400 dancers who just could not stop. Dozens died from exhaustion, heart attack or stroke. The plague lasted a month.[12]

The historian John Waller, who studied historical records of the time, noted that 'anxiety and false fears gripped the region'[13] concerning famine and financial worries, but notably including the Catholic fear of the Sicilian martyr, St Vitus, who is invoked as a protection against epilepsy. Anyone who invoked the wrath of St Vitus, it was known, would be sent a plague of compulsive dancing.

Mass psychogenic illnesses from 1980s onwards have been more appropriate for the fears of our time. We don't dance any more, but suffer from illnesses which mirror the symptoms of chemical attacks or food poisoning. According to research, typical symptoms from 1980 to 1990 were headache (present in 67 per cent of documented cases), dizziness (46 per cent), nausea (41 per cent) and stomach pains (39 per cent).[14] In the modern world of terrorist threats, it is no surprise that MSI episodes are dominated by fears of chemicals, smells, etc.

One outbreak of mass psychogenic illness occurred in a small village in Lebanon in 2006. Eight people were admitted to hospital in Beirut with shortness of breath, muscle cramps, tremors and dizziness. Of course, initial thoughts were of infection, or even 'bio-terrorism', especially because the village was threatened by war. Eventually, the diagnosis was mass psychogenic illness and effective strategies were then put in place to contain it.[15]

Just like a biologically infectious disease, each episode of MSI is highly contagious and spreads from person to person. Outbreaks tend to occur much more in isolated groups where people are tightly interconnected than in a typical city. Common locations include schools, factories or even small villages. Around half of all outbreaks over the 20-year period from 1973 to 1993 were in schools, 29 per cent were in factories and 10 per cent in towns and villages.[16]

Mass psychogenic illnesses tend to be spread by those who are overly worried about things and who have exaggerated fears, say, of terrorism or food poisoning. Children and young adolescents seem to be particularly susceptible to catching such illnesses, and women are affected more than men. Fear, stress and anxiety in a group seem to be the triggers.

The outbreak usually starts with just one person whose symptoms require medical attention. They typically report that they smelled something. The fear then spreads from mind to mind, from one vulnerable person to the next. As it spreads, other people report smelling something. The smell has probably always been there but nobody has really noticed it before. But now their senses are heightened and people can definitely pick it out. Or their brain can conjure it up.

Soon the nocebo effect kicks in big style and people are getting headaches, feeling faint and even passing out. Now the anxiety is really spreading. I mean, people are passing out. But this only raises the grip of the nocebo effect. Within a short time dozens, if not hundreds, of people are experiencing headaches, dizziness, nausea and stomach cramps.

Bacteria and viruses are not involved, but this doesn't mean these symptoms are 'all in the mind'. There is no such thing as 'all in the mind'. You cannot think something without causing a change in the brain and body. Researchers studying the placebo effect for analgesics, anti-depressants and anti-Parkinson's medicines have shown that believing you are receiving a drug produces many of the same neural changes as the drugs they are paired against.[17]

There may be a link between the spread of a mass psychogenic illness and mirror neurons. At least that's the belief outlined in a 2010 paper in the journal *Medical Hypotheses*.[18] Part of the mirror neuron system inhibits action, which prevents us from automatically copying everything we see. Without this our arms would move involuntarily every time we saw someone move their arm. The authors of the paper suggest that this inhibitive part of the mirror neuron system might not be functioning as well in people who are affected by mass psychogenic illness and thus they have little control over copying others. This might also have been the case with the dancing plague.

And what about 'flu? There have been a few 'pandemic' reports of 'flu – bird 'flu and swine 'flu – that have involved the obvious spread of the viruses. But fear has also spread and it's almost impossible not to consider that the intensity of some people's symptoms has been more to do with fear than with the actual virus.

And therefore, among the statistics of the pandemics lies a percentage of people (I have no idea how many) who were infected more with fear than 'flu.

If they did catch the 'flu, or even a bad cold, this would have ensured that their symptoms were much worse than they'd ordinarily be. The stress from the fear would have weakened their immune system and made them more vulnerable to the virus.

In any situation where there is high public anxiety on account of substantial media coverage of a 'pandemic', there will almost certainly be a percentage of the population infected with mass psychogenic illness rather than the illness itself. Indeed, a 2009 study reported heightened public anxiety during the initial stages of swine 'flu, which would have provided a fertile psychological ground for the spread of fear.[19]

$$*****$$

So we know that fear can spread. Fortunately it is likely that its opposite – courage – can also spread.

Interesting research shows that we might be able to immunize ourselves against acquiring fear from others. Further research at the University of Wisconsin near Madison found that when monkeys spent six sessions first observing a monkey showing no fear of snakes and then later observing six sessions of monkeys behaving fearfully with snakes, six out of eight of them did not develop a fear of snakes.[20]

When a person acts with courage, others are inspired and become stronger.

Nelson Mandela said, 'I learned that courage was not the absence of fear, but the triumph over it. The brave man is not he who does not feel afraid, but he who conquers that fear.'[21]

Perhaps if we learn courage, we will immunize ourselves against catching fear and all that comes with it. Courage does not mean we should be irresponsible, but that we should be intelligent, especially when it comes to the fear of an epidemic.

Intelligent courage paves the way for sensible action and allows fear to be transmuted. Then its contagiousness is halted and it is prevented from infecting others.

# CHAPTER 11

# THE POWER OF POSITIVE PEOPLE

## 'Oh, give us the man who sings at his work.'

Thomas Carlyle

One obvious place where mood contagion affects us is at our place of work, because people spend a lot of time together in the workplace. Research now shows that emotions travel very efficiently there.

This can have obvious positive effects because one or two group members can elevate the mood of others. From a business perspective, this increases group performance.

This was shown in a Yale University study involving 94 undergraduate business students randomly assigned as heads of departments. Their task was to negotiate bonus money for employees in their departments from a limited overall budget. Each head was to represent a member of their staff and had to secure the best possible bonus from the group pot. But at the same time they had to co-operate with the committee to make the best use of the money in the pot to benefit the whole company. To top off the exercise, they were told that if they didn't reach an agreement within the given time, no one would get a bonus at all.

The Yale researchers planted an actor in each group who was asked to either be pleasant (happy, warm, optimistic and either cheerfully enthusiastic or pleasantly calm) or unpleasant (hostile, pessimistic, irritable and either energetically unpleasant or sluggish and dull).

To measure emotional contagion, the researchers had each participant fill out a questionnaire that identified their mood at the start of the experiment and then again at the end. Their facial expressions were also secretly monitored throughout as indicators of mood.

At the end of the task, following analysis of facial expressions and the questionnaire, it was clear that the moods of the participants who were in the group with the pleasant actor were more positive at the end than they had been at the start. Those in the group with the unpleasant actor were more negative than they had been at the start. The overall mood of the group was also rated as positive when the actor was pleasant but negative when the actor was unpleasant. One person's mood had an impact on each team member and also on the group as a whole. It had a ripple effect.

And the type of ripple affected performance. Where the actor was pleasant there was much more co-operation and agreement between department heads, and their overall performance relative to the unpleasant actor's group was better. When the actor was unpleasant, there was more conflict within the group.

The author of the study concluded that people are 'walking mood inductors' who are 'continuously influencing the moods and then the judgements and behaviours of others'.[1]

This shows that in small teams, even one positive or negative person can sway the mood of the whole group and affect the group performance. Performance is affected because when we're in a good mood, our judgement is good. But when we're stressed or in a bad mood, our judgement can be impaired.

Because we often have to work so closely with others, the way we feel in groups and teams has as much to do with the emotional state of the other members as it has to do with our own state. This was the conclusion of a 2010 study which involved 48 work groups. The researchers found that it was especially true for negative emotions but less so for positive ones. Their own personality accounted for 31 per cent in their variance of positive emotion, and the effect of others accounted for 10 per cent. For negative emotion, their own personality accounted for 19 per cent of their variance, but the presence of others accounted for 23 per cent.[2]

The plus side is that when we're happy we're less affected by others. But when we're not, we're more susceptible to the contagiousness of negative emotions.

I once worked with a group of people where one member had, unbeknownst to him, been labelled a 'chaos agent'. I noticed that the accuracy of this description actually depended on what kind of mood he was in. When he was in a good mood, the meetings were high energy, creative and productive, and everyone left on a high, but when he was in a bad mood then chaos was a pretty accurate description. Hardly anything was accomplished at these times. It was mostly just conflict.

Actors talk of the same thing on film sets. If an actor or director or someone senior is in a bad mood and expresses it on set, it can affect the whole cast and crew and nobody performs at their best. The implications of this, based on research in business teams, is that a film's quality could suffer. But when a positive mood spreads throughout a set, actors, cast and crew will be at their best and pull out all the stops to make a great movie.

Another study showed that positive mood improved creative problem-solving. In the study, conducted at the University of Maryland, participants had a positive mood induced in them either through watching a section of a comedy film or being given a bag of sweets. Then they performed better in two separate tasks that required creative ingenuity than control or negative mood groups.[3]

Since then many studies have linked positive emotion with improved problem-solving and creativity, so when it spreads in a group it is good for business.

It is also known that people who experience positive emotions set higher goals and have a higher expectancy of achievement. In a 2005 study, scientists at Michigan State University and the University of Florida showed that people adjusted their goals downward when they experienced negative emotion and upward when they experienced positive emotion.[4]

Other research shows that happy moods promote group performance much better than sad moods.[5] Happy moods improve people's ability to broaden their focus to a wide range of information and resources. I think most people will agree that we are definitely more productive when we feel good.

Co-operation is important for productivity but also for job satisfaction and the mental health of team members. Lots of research has shown that when a person is in a positive mood it encourages kindness (helping behaviour) and co-operation and reduces aggression.[6]

When we're in a positive mood, we are also more creative and use more of the information available to us. This has been experimentally shown to be true. In a 2007 study, for instance, volunteers used much more available information from cues supplied by a Decision Support System (DSS).[7] When we draw upon more resources, we have more information and make better decisions. What should be of interest to senior business leaders io that this leads to better competitive ability, greater company effectiveness and therefore bigger profits.

Where a positive mood is especially important is in a clinical environment, where doctors routinely make decisions that affect the lives of their patients. In a Cornell University study of positive emotion and diagnosis times involving 44 internists, those who had a positive mood induced in them as part of the study made a diagnosis of liver disease much faster than those in a control group.[8]

We mostly think of groups and teams in a business setting, but there are many different kinds of teams. Emotions are also contagious in healthcare teams. A 2009 study at Sunnybrook Health Sciences Center in Toronto examined the impact of stress on the performance of health professionals (physicians, residents and respiratory therapists) in a busy ICU. They found that if a patient's condition deteriorated unexpectedly or resources were not sufficiently available, situations that caused a sudden increase in stress and anxiety in one of the professionals, it would spread throughout the rest of the group.[9]

Clearly, any way of generating or spreading positive emotion in a company or organization has benefit. One or two positive or happy people in a team can bring great rewards. Obviously, we can't have a situation where only happy people are employed and I'm sure we have all known people who weren't exactly the happiest at work but nevertheless did a great job. But it might be something for managers to bear in mind when thinking of team dynamics.

## THE BOTTOM LINE

What does the contagiousness of positive or negative emotions actually mean for businesses? Can it be put into monetary terms? It turns out it can.

We tend to think of frontline staff as having the greatest impact upon customer satisfaction and spending, but research is beginning to consider the effect of the manager's moods on these staff.

A 2010 report, for instance, collected data from a single retail chain that sold women's clothing and accessories. The study included 306 store managers, 1,615 frontline staff and 57,656 customers, and showed that how satisfied the store manager felt in their job impacted how satisfied customers were and even how much they spent, even though the store manager had much less contact with customers than the frontline staff did.

In monetary terms, for each point increase in manager satisfaction (on a seven-point scale) there was a 5.07 per cent increase in customer spending, which equated to each customer spending $3.64 more every time they visited the store.

The researchers concluded, 'These results suggest that managers may set the tone for customer satisfaction and store performance.'[10]

Of course, a manager's satisfaction affects their job performance and this will have an obvious bearing on store performance too, but in light of the information presented here, we can say with some degree of certainty that it is not just what a manager *does* that matters, but how they *feel*.

When Elizabeth was 16 years old, she worked part-time in a clothing store. When the manager was in a good mood – which wasn't very often! – the staff were more relaxed and cheerful, which I guess would have made the customers enjoy being there, soaking up a positive mood as they looked upon smiling faces on the staff. But when the manager was her usual grumpy self, the staff were more stilted and slightly nervous. In fact one time, Elizabeth recalls, a customer approached the manager and told her that she should speak to the staff in a 'nicer' manner. Then the customer left, looking quite angry.

## LEADER MOOD TRANSMISSION

The idea that leaders influence emotions in a group is not a new one. In 1942, the psychoanalyst Fritz Redl concluded that groups had emotion (what we now call 'group affective tone') and that leaders influenced it.[11]

Group affective tone can be considered the typical emotional reaction of a group and thus not all groups have an affective tone, as some are more splintered. You might think of it as people all 'singing off the same hymn sheet', so to speak, which is typical of groups who spend regular time together. These tend to be homogeneous in their individual moods.

A leader in any organization has a very important role – not only the obvious one of managing staff and ensuring that projects are completed, but also the role of maintaining a positive mood within their team. Their own mood plays a part in this. A 2005 study showed that a leader's mood was passed onto those who reported to them and also affected the overall group affective tone.[12]

The study involved 189 students (107 women and 82 men) who worked together in various-sized self-management groups. None of them knew the real purpose of the study. Instead they were told that it was to do with a memory recall task around setting up a tent.

A leader was selected for each group and was given information on what the group would be doing, although they were not told the real purpose of the study either. They were shown a video clip, either a positive or negative one, and told that their recall ability would be tested after they had built the tent. The positive mood clip was a funny clip of David Letterman and the negative clip was part of a documentary about social injustice. The purpose here was to induce either a positive or negative mood in the leaders. They filled out a mood questionnaire immediately after watching the clip.

The leaders then joined the rest of their group and they worked together for seven minutes to plan their strategy for building the tents. After this, the team members also filled out a mood questionnaire.

Then the teams set about the task of building their tents while blindfolded. The researchers chose blindfolding because it is known that blindfolded participants behave more naturally and are less self-conscious than normal, so it was a good way to study how the team members interacted.

Mood was again measured on completion of the task.

It was found that after the seven minutes of interacting and planning their strategies, the moods of the team members who -

had a leader who had been exposed to the positive clip were more positive than those who were with a leader who had been shown the negative emotion clip. And the same pattern was found after building the tent.

Overall affective tone was also higher in the 'positive' group than in the 'negative' group after the seven-minute planning stage and after the tent-building exercise.

And when the researchers studied the individual groups carrying out their tasks, the scientists concluded that the groups who had had the positive mood leaders had expended much less effort and been significantly more co-ordinated than the groups who had had the negative mood leaders.

This was also shown in a 1995 experiment involving 53 sales managers who were leaders of groups ranging in size from four to nine people. The study found that the leader's mood affected not only the performance of individual members of the team but also the performance of the team as a whole. It also affected the satisfaction level of the team members. And, furthermore, the leader's own manager impacted their mood. In other words, the mood at the top of the pyramid affected all of those at the base.[13]

So, the mood at the top affects the satisfaction levels of employees. And we want satisfied employees. Sears used an 'employee-customer-profit chain' to work out what impact the attitudes the employees had towards their jobs and towards the company had on profits. They used information from 800 stores and found that employee attitudes impacted their behaviour towards customers. But, crucially, they found that each 5 per cent increase in employee satisfaction produced a 1.3 per cent increase in customer satisfaction, and this resulted in a 0.5 per cent increase in revenue growth.[14]

In summary, the emotional environment created in an organization impacts its profits. I call this EP – Environment to Profit.

The emotional environment impacts the feelings of employees, which impacts the emotions they transmit to customers, which affects how the customers evaluate the service quality, which has a bearing on the profits of the organization.

Senior leaders must strive to find a way to build a positive environment in a company so that leaders and staff are positively affected. It might be, for instance, that they create an inspiring vision that also incorporates social benefits to society, or find a fair financial or responsibility structure.

## WHEN MOODS CONVERGE

There is a great deal of evidence that shows that the moods of individuals in teams affect each other and that, in time, there is a gradual process of mood convergence where people's average mood becomes similar. Think of it like the mixing of different colour droplets of dye in water. In time the colours will have mixed and the water will have its own hue, or tone – the group affective tone.

The convergence of moods within teams is well known. In one study, for instance, 65 community nurses who were part of 13 separate teams were asked to record their moods and hassles every day for three weeks. Afterwards there was a significant association between the moods of individual nurses and the collective moods of their teams that was independent of the effects of any external events. Their moods really did mix.

Interestingly, the most mood convergence was shown with older nurses who were highly committed to the team – in other words, where there was a greater sense of interconnectedness. This is consistent with everything we have learned so far. The more connected we feel, the more we share our emotions.

In the researchers' view, 'The findings suggest that people's mood at work can become linked to the mood of their teammates.'[15]

The same process occurs in sports teams and evidence shows that it undoubtedly affects the outcome of matches.

This was shown in a study of players from two professional cricket teams appropriately entitled 'Catching Moods and Hitting Runs'.[16] The players were each given pocket computers and were asked to record their mood and their performances four times a day over four days during a competitive match between the two teams.

Analysis showed significant correlation between the players' own happy moods, the average collective mood of the team and their perceived performances. And these were not related to hassles or actual standings in the match. The mood convergence was highest when the players were happy and working collectively. Their happy climates mixed.

And just like the nurses, the highest mood linkage was with older players who were most committed to the team.

Being committed to a team is known to raise emotional contagion. And it affects the outcome of games. This was effectively shown in a 2010 study of penalty shootouts in international football matches. Scientists from the University of Groningen in the Netherlands watched videos of penalty shootouts in 151 World Cup and European Championship football games (all of the games from the 1974–2006 World Cups and the 1972 and 2008 European Championships) – a total of 325 penalty kicks – and rated displays of positive emotions in the teams.

They found that players who were more positive in their celebratory displays were more likely to be in the team that won the shootout. They typically showed pride (arms up, pumping fists, expanded chest) or joy (wide smile). Specifically, celebrations involving both arms (which amounted to around two thirds of the players who scored their penalties) were associated with winning.

The researchers also noted that when such a display was made it was more likely that the next player from the other team missed than when no such display was made.

And players who looked down after scoring were more likely to end up on the losing side.[17]

Importantly it is celebrations with other team members that matter most and not 'in your face'-type mocking of the other team, which really only fires the other side up.

From 1997 to 1999 I was manager of the junior men's team (aged 17–20) of Sale Harriers Manchester athletics club, one of the UK's largest athletic clubs. In my first season as manager, we reached the UK championship finals and came third. One thing about that final that always stuck in my mind was that the team that won that year (Blackheath Harriers) had incredible team spirit and a lot of supporters. They sang and celebrated every performance, which really seemed to boost the spirits of the athletes. Many of the individual performances that day were personal bests and I was convinced that their collective spirit helped them win that day.

So the following year I tried a little experiment. I realized that the team I was managing wasn't as strong as it had been the previous year because some of our best athletes had moved up to the senior ranks. In my view, it would take a few seasons to build the same strength again. We weren't likely to reach the UK championship finals that year (although we did!). So I volunteered to help out in the finals in the young athletes age group, which runs from young kids right up to the age of 16.

We had a very strong young athletes team that year and I made a point of doing all that I could to boost team spirit and individual performances. I spoke to as many athletes as I could before and after their event, congratulating them on good efforts and performances and making an effort to say something positive no matter where they finished. Team spirit was high and gradually built up throughout the day. And Sale Harriers Young Athletes were crowned UK champions that day.

Of course, I am by no means attempting to take credit for the victory. The performance of the individual athletes, the work by individual coaches throughout the season, and an excellent team manager (John Smith) contributed most to the victory that day. But team spirit may also have played a part.

## WHEN WE CALL CUSTOMER SERVICE

Most people, when they phone the customer service department of a business, do so to complain. It's easy to imagine the effect of this: customer service workers can be very susceptible to emotional contagion, and since the mood being transmitted is usually negative (angry, aggressive) this can affect their health, leading to stress and even burnout.

This was shown in a study that was aptly titled 'The Influence of Angry Customer Outbursts on Service Providers' Facial Displays and Affective States'. In the study, 192 volunteers played the role of customer service staff (94 men and 98 women) and each volunteer was selected on the basis that they had recent frontline service experience in dealing with customers, so they were believed to represent typical customer service staff. They were shown videos of either angry or non-angry customers complaining about lost airline luggage and were given the fake cover story that the researchers wanted to investigate their verbal responses to customer complaints, thereby diverting their attention from what they were really doing, which was studying their facial expressions for emotional contagion.

The results clearly showed that the volunteers who had watched the angry videos displayed many more negative facial expressions than those who had watched videos of non-angry customers. For instance, 87.9 per cent of the volunteers who had watched the angry complaint displayed 'negative smiles' compared with only 9.1 per cent of those who had watched the non-angry complaint. Rapid blinking was seen in 18.7 per cent of those who had seen the angry complaint compared with only 1.1 per cent of those who had seen the non-angry one. On the other hand, 76.2 per cent of the latter volunteers showed positive smiles but only 28.6 per cent of those who had seen the angry complaint showed any positive smiles.[18]

These kinds of displays might seem pretty obvious. Of course we're going to feel anxious or angry when someone vents at us. But we now know from research in mirror neurons and emotional contagion that we're not *just* feeling anxious or angry because of what they *said*, but because of what they were *feeling*.

And transmitted anxiety or anger is not short-lived. If someone is angry with you, do you shake it off within a couple of seconds or does it affect you for the rest of the day? Anger usually stays with us for a while because our nervous system is affected. We produce extra adrenaline, which can take time to leave our body. Customer service staff have to deal with this every day: more than 20 per cent of all customer service calls involve angry outbursts.[19]

It has been my experience that when you're nice to customer service staff you stand a far higher chance of getting your complaint resolved than if you're angry. It's not their fault that you're not happy.

Also, the person on the phone or behind the counter is another human being with their own worries and concerns. Some of them are parents who look after young children who they love very much. They've probably already had dozens of people that week shouting at them. If you consider this, you might be a little calmer as you communicate.

I'm not suggesting that you don't complain, but there are many different ways to complain without getting angry.

Some people adopt the stance that customer service employees are trained to deal with anger, but in my opinion this is no excuse for being nasty to them and playing the bully. We can convince ourselves that we're justified in being angry, but this doesn't change the fact that we are being unkind to someone.

I recently heard about a girl who was happily sitting at her customer service desk in a large store. Then a man approached and asked if she could sell him something there. She said that she was sorry, but she wasn't allowed to. He stormed off, only to return a few minutes later shouting, 'Terrible! Pathetic!' The girl looked teary afterwards and was very shy with customers for the rest of the day.

Despite their training, customer service staff are not immune to emotional contagion. Picking up negative emotion is mostly involuntary and, in my experience, remaining unaffected usually requires an understanding of emotional contagion.

Awareness of emotional contagion must in fact lead us to learn better ways to communicate. Next time you are really satisfied with a product or service, why not call customer services and tell them so? You might just make someone's day.

I once saw a woman come into a shop and hand an assistant a box of chocolates for being so helpful to her. She was obviously returning from being in the shop earlier. The assistant was taken aback – in a good way – and it put a smile on my face and that of everyone else who was there at the time.

## CHARISMA

Team members are not only inspired by the people they come into contact with, but by charismatic leaders. Such leaders can be highly efficient transmitters of positive emotion.

In a 2001 experiment, college students were defined as charismatic when they showed intense smiling and paid frequent attention to the audience during simulated campaign speeches. Observation of the audience during the speeches of these 'charismatic leaders' showed that they were mimicking the facial expressions of the speaker much more than when non-charismatic speakers took to the stage. And when you mimic someone's facial expression, you feel the same emotion as they do, as we have seen. So the charismatic leaders transmitted their emotions more powerfully than the non-charismatic leaders.[20]

In another part of the experiment, observers watched excerpts of the first 1992 presidential debate between Bill Clinton and George Bush Sr. And they mimicked Clinton's charismatic facial expressions. And, as we know, Bill Clinton became president.

Compare this with the difficulties faced by ex-prime minister Gordon Brown. Despite his accomplishments, people always wanted him to be more outgoing and smile more. His often depressed expression and downbeat tones did not inspire Britain, especially compared with his predecessor, Tony Blair, a charismatic leader. People like a leader who instils them with confidence and a charismatic leader can do that because they project their own positive emotion. A non-charismatic leader might be doing exactly the same job or even a better one, but people believe in a charismatic leader more because they feel positive while listening to that leader. And so they vote for them.

When Gordon Brown left office, he was filmed leaving 10 Downing Street with his wife and children, and for a few moments the nation saw a different side to him, a genuinely emotionally expressive side. And you know what? People liked him more. 'Why didn't he show this in the election?' was a typical comment. 'He might have won!'

It's a bit like talent shows. A less talented contestant can go a lot further than a more talented singer if they are likeable, or if they have a personal story that inspires empathy. Suddenly we feel a connection with them and like them better.

In another study, 103 leaders (mostly middle managers with two levels above them and four levels below them) were sent a questionnaire to fill out themselves, a 'leader questionnaire', and another to be filled out by three people who directly reported to them, a 'follower questionnaire'. The follower questionnaire contained items that were known to provide a reliable measure of the leader's charisma.

In the 'leader questionnaire', each leader was asked to write their vision statement as a set of 'core principles, beliefs, and goals that guide behaviour' for their work group. This vision was then analysed for emotional content and its positive tone determined by the number of positive emotional words contained in it.

Comparing the two questionnaires, it was clear that charismatic leaders were the ones who expressed the most positive emotion.[21]

In a second part of the study, 71 leaders were videotaped giving presentations. Analysis of their facial expressions also linked charisma with the expression of positive emotion.

The researchers ranked the 71 videotapes according to how much positive emotion the leaders had expressed. Then, choosing the four leaders who had expressed the most positive emotion (i.e. the most charismatic leaders), they combined their presentations to produce a single video of 'high leader positive affect'. Similarly, they created a single video of 'low leader positive affect' from the four lowest rated videos.

One hundred and thirty-three undergraduate psychology students (69 per cent female and 31 per cent male) then watched the videos and reported their mood at the start and at the end.

Those who watched the high leader videos ended up being in a more positive mood afterwards than the group who watched the low leader videos. The students also rated the leaders in the high positive group to be more effective.

William J. Kerr is the professor who supervised my PhD. He is a charismatic leader. When he was in a positive state he uplifted our whole group (the 'Kerr Group', as it was known), and magic occurred: for the rest of the day, quality results would flow out of our lab. It was as though everything we touched turned to gold. 'Billy' put much of the group's success down to the high-quality students who worked in the lab and probably never realized the big part that his own personality played in it.

# HOW TO TRANSMIT POSITIVE EMOTION IN A SPEECH

We can use this knowledge about the benefits of transmitting positive emotion to uplift and inspire our audience when we are giving a presentation or speech. Whenever I'm speaking in a room or venue that isn't very well set up – that's, say, a little dark, or the position of the chairs makes things chaotic, or there's something else about the venue that dampens the atmosphere – I set myself the goal of turning the mood around. The way I do this is to make upward tweaks to my expressiveness.

To give a really good presentation, you also really need to believe in what you are saying, otherwise the audience will pick up from non-verbal signals that you're not entirely in agreement with what you are saying or you don't totally understand it yourself. When you believe what you are saying, the audience will believe it. And if you think it's really important, your non-verbal expressions will help them to think it's very important too.

This is why leaders can reach a level of great influence even when they're promoting destructive ideas. If they believe something is right, however misguided they are, people will pick up on their belief and passion and be seduced by their ideas. This helped Hitler come to power.

Belief and passion are really effective. When a speaker is personally moved, their audience will be moved too. If it's just words to them, it will just be words to the audience too. It is believed that at least 60–65 per cent of what a person really puts across is conveyed non-verbally.[22]

One challenge here is that when you are facing a sceptical audience, you might pick up on many of their non-verbal signals of disapproval and it can overwhelm your own expressions. It really comes down to who is more expressive. Ultimately, as the presenter, it really is down to you. So exaggerate your expressiveness if you have to. Use your physiology to perk up your positive emotion.

*****

A good leader can use their positive mood to inspire people. They don't need to be charismatic – charisma is a booster to positive emotion, but there are many leaders who move people through their honesty, kindness and sincerity and make them feel good about themselves.

Mark Twain wrote, 'Keep away from people who try to belittle your ambitions. Small people always do that, but the really great make you feel that you, too, can become great.'[23]

Keeping a person down is detrimental to all of us. Only when each person is allowed to fly do we all fly. That is the nature of interconnectedness.

And through that interconnectedness, moods travel like a current along a wire, infecting everyone in the network. If the mood is positive then everyone is lifted and creativity flourishes.

# CHAPTER 12

# THERE'S POWER IN YOUR FACE

'Let's not forget that the little emotions are the great captains of our lives and we obey them without even realizing it.'

Vincent van Gogh

We can turn emotional contagion to good use in peacemaking. If we can hold onto an inner state of relaxation then we can pass this on in an environment of conflict and bring some peace to the atmosphere.

Just one person can make a difference. A friend of mine who is part of a meditation group tells me that the group meditations are always better quality when a particular person is there. When they are absent, the meditations don't seem to have the same depth.

When you are aiming to bring some peace to a situation, one asset is your breathing. Breathe slowly, moderately deeply, steadily and easily. This will have an impact upon your overall physiology, your autonomic nervous system, your emotional state and eventually your mind. And as your mind and body become calm, you will project this outwards, infecting those around you with a state of physiological and mental peace.

## WHY IT'S BETTER TO SEE SOMEONE

If you want peace to be contagious, it's better to communicate face to face. Any type of negotiation is much more powerful when it's face to face than when it's over the telephone or by email, because only by being face to face can you transmit your state. Of course, little emoticons can make a difference because they indicate the intentions behind a sentence, but there is no substitute for face-to-face communication for making peace because you can use all of your non-verbal powers. That way, it takes less time and fewer words.

Face-to-face communication is important because it gives us the opportunity to create rapport. As a peacemaker, you must be the source of this rapport. You can mirror a person's body language and this will help you to connect with them. They will like you more. Then you can start to make subtle shifts to your own expressions to convey a sense of peace and this will start to bring them to a more relaxed state too.

The efficacy of face-to-face communication in a conflict situation was experimentally tested by Stanford researchers Aimée Drolet and Michael Morris. In a simulated strike negotiation, they placed some negotiators face to face and others side by side and found that the face-to-face negotiators agreed on a settlement early in the strike and much more quickly than those who were side by side.[1]

Much research has shown that negotiators often fail and this results in expensive delays and more anger and acrimony between people and groups, so finding out that face-to-face communication is the most optimal social and psychological process for conflict resolution is important.

Many situations in life can bring forth mixed motives. We might have a desire for a peaceful resolution to a conflict but have our own self-interests too. Even when one party tries to resolve the conflict because they understand that it will be less costly and more beneficial to everyone, they often have their own agenda and might only want to co-operate if the other side co-operates. But someone has to make the first move for both parties to co-operate. Here again non-verbal communication can be valuable.

It can be also beneficial when we are entertaining a prospective client or business leader. With face-to-face communication, we give ourselves the opportunity to convey our personal belief in the product or service and our capacity to deliver. This belief will be contagious to the prospective client, even when we have little track record, and they will develop a positive feeling about us, which will massively increase our odds of working with them.

This is why business leaders and diplomats would rather travel halfway around the world to have a short conversation face to face than discuss matters over the phone or by email. Even though it can be costly in terms of time and expense, the benefits of a swifter deal and a stronger future relationship far outweigh the costs. People can create rapport and develop a strong enough liking to transcend many of the details of a disagreement.

Face-to-face communication has always made sense to me and been my preferred method of operating. In the last year that I worked in the pharmaceutical industry, I moved out of the labs completely and had a project management role – which in some of my projects was actually more of a conflict resolution role.

The job was a very large career step-up for me and I owe a debt of gratitude to the team leader, John Stephens, for deciding to recruit a complete rookie instead of someone much more qualified for the role. John's reasoning, and he turned out to be correct, was that in not having the required experience for the job (5–10 years in a sales and marketing or project management role; I had three years in a lab), I would bring a fresh way of thinking to the team of project managers.

The way things were traditionally done in the team was that the internal system allowed you to access everyone else's diary and you could then select a time for a meeting. This would send an automatic meeting request to the person which they could accept or decline.

I didn't see the sense of that. In the labs, if you wanted something you'd just go and ask for it. It had been the same when I'd done my PhD – if you wanted to borrow equipment, you wouldn't think twice about walking to a different building to ask for it. If we had sent emails or meeting requests, it would have taken ages. In the labs, if you needed something, you kind of needed it there and then.

So I carried on that way in the project management team. I never once used the expensive software system. I much preferred to walk halfway across the site and knock on a door, even if it took me half an hour. And if the person wasn't in, I'd have a wee walk around looking for them, and often make other connections in the process.

This way of working seemed like time-wasting to some, but by developing relationships through face-to-face communication I was able to develop much less 'professional' and more casual relationships with 'stakeholders' in the teams that I worked with. And through emotional contagion they would have sensed my genuine desire to help them.

A side-effect of this was that people were much more willing to help me out when I had a problem, and meetings were much more relaxed. They were still efficient, though. We would often tie up more business in five minutes than I saw some other project teams accomplish in two weeks. Where there are strong personal relationships, people are much more willing to go that extra half-mile, even if it is an inconvenience to them.

I actually remember on more than one occasion spending 55 minutes of an hour's meeting just chatting about nothing really of any substance – telling some jokes, laughing and talking about general stuff and then looking at my watch and saying, 'Oops, look at the time. We'd better get some work done.' Then we'd take a pretty big step forward on the project in those last five minutes.

At one point it came to light that I had several more active projects than the other team members, due to some little projects that I had picked up along the way. A few weeks later, at my annual review, John gave me some feedback that had been given by some of the senior stakeholders in my projects: they couldn't understand how I accomplished so much in such short amounts of time. I actually wondered what took others so long.

If only they'd known how little 'work' I actually did, in the classic sense of the word! There were times when I'd arrive in the morning and spend the entire day just walking about the site talking to people, not attending a single project meeting or reading a single email. But, in hindsight, what I was actually doing was much more important: I was building relationships through face-to-face contact and, as I enjoyed that contact, I was spreading a positive mood to each person I was communicating with.

It's funny, but it was in that relatively high-level professional job that I learned some of my best jokes – and made sure they spread about the site of course.

Face-to-face communication allows people to relate to one another and understand one another better, and allows emotions (and jokes) to flow from person to person. It allows one person's positive mood to infect another person or one person's troubles to give another the chance to show empathy. It sets the scene for breakthroughs in a working environment as barriers between people are dropped.

## TEASING THE BEST OUT OF PEOPLE

Have you ever met someone who just seems to be lucky? It seems to me that we can make people luckier when we think of them like that. We can even make a person communicate better or jam up inside, depending on the non-verbal signals we're transmitting to them.

If a person thinks you are something special, their view will come out in their subtle facial expressions, in their body language, in their eyes, and not just in what they say but in *how* they say it. If they want you to succeed at something, this will subtly affect how you behave, bringing about tiny adjustments in how you perform.

A presenter can give a better talk or a comedian on stage can give a better performance if the audience holds them in high esteem. The audience's positive signals are contagious to them and therefore they 'flow' better.

Similarly, if someone would rather you fail, their tension will bring out tension in you too. Their thoughts about you are contagious.

This was experimentally demonstrated in a 1986 study where men were asked to phone women they thought were either attractive or homely, according to the brief they had been given. The women did vary in appearance. But the interesting thing is that they became more like the idea the men had of them.

For instance, when the men thought they were attractive, they became more confident, animated and even humorous. They were also quite comfortable on the phone. And when the men thought they were homely, they were more withdrawn and showed less confidence. They were also much more awkward on the phone.[2]

In a very real sense a person embodies our thoughts about them. Even if we're not saying what we really think, they can detect this in our voice, or in our eyes, or in a subtle body shift, or even get an intuitive sense because their mirror neurons pick up a very brief flash of emotion. So their behaviour can then follow what we expect of them, or even what we hope for them.

Several years ago, my friend Jamie and I were in a pub where a group of local lads was playing pool. One of them was a real pool shark and was the local champion. We didn't know that at the time. Thinking they could make some money, they invited us to have a game with them. I was a bit reluctant, but Jamie accepted for us before I could open my mouth.

On my first visit to the table, I accidentally played an awesome shot. In that situation, normally I'd go in for a high five and soak up the credit, but I didn't know the guys we were playing with, so I played it completely cool. To them it looked as though I'd meant it. I ended up in great position and potted a few more balls.

On my next visit to the table, I made another great shot – another total fluke.

As the game went on, it seemed as though every shot I played was guided by magic. I ended up having one of the luckiest runs ever, with more flukes than I'd ever had in a game. I easily won the first game, and the money.

The shark was stunned. I could see his friends looking at him as if to say, 'How did that happen?' They were convinced that I was a really lucky player, one of those people who would land on their feet if they fell out of an aeroplane. But that worked for me, as it helped me to be even luckier.

They insisted we play another game and again I had a really lucky run. You could have sworn someone was invisibly guiding the balls or controlling my cue arm. Jamie and I couldn't believe my luck.

After a few more games, the shark had had enough. I had cleaned up in the financial stakes. His pride wasn't exactly hurt – he accepted defeat by calling me the 'jammiest' person he'd ever played. I don't think he could accept that it was anything to do with skill.

A week or so later, Jamie and I were back in the pub, but this time we were playing darts. Not being great darts players, we were stuck trying to get a double one to win the game. With darts, you start on 501 points and every score you make with your three darts is subtracted. To win the game you have to finish on a double. If you hit the single accidentally, you have to hit a lower double. So if you're a pretty bad player, you'll keep hitting the single and have to go for lower and lower doubles until you end up having to hit the double one to win. Some players can be stuck there for ages and on that day those players were us. It was a bit of a joke really. We just could not hit the double one.

After what seemed like an age, the pool shark shouted over to us. He'd been watching us play from the doorway and had concluded that my lucky run had well and truly long gone. He offered us a rematch at pool.

Once again, Jamie accepted on our behalf. I think he just needed a reason to put the darts down. I had started to walk towards the pool table, which was in the next room, when he shouted over, 'David, the dart!' I hadn't realized that I was still holding one of the darts. Now, at least six or seven yards away from the board, I quickly glanced around and casually threw the dart towards the board with a little flick of my wrist.

Well, what do you know? It went straight into the double one.

The shark just threw his hands in the air. I could see stress, disbelief and total frustration on his face. He refused to play pool with me after that.

At least I won the darts game.

I can't take the full credit, of course. The shark, and Jamie, had expected me to be lucky, and I was. It seems to me that their thoughts and beliefs about me impacted their subtle expressions and body language, which in turn impacted my muscles so that I played exactly as they expected me to.

Setting luck aside, we also bring out positive behaviour in people. When we focus on a person's good qualities, we tease more of these qualities out. In a sense we get more of what we concentrate on.

Knowing that a person has the ability to be calm, for instance, can tease this out of them. The peace that we see in them, even though it might not be staring us in the face, makes us adjust our own subtle facial and body language and this is then transmitted to them. In time, they move towards what we have focused on.

It works the same with kindness, warmth, compassion and even positivity.

So why not, just for today, try to see the best in people? Make an effort to look past any negative attitudes and behaviour and think of them in more life-enhancing ways.

It may sound pretty idealistic, but I honestly believe that seeing the best in people can make a difference in the world.

# YOU CAN'T RESIST A SMILE

### 'A smile is a curve that sets everything straight.'
Phyllis Dyer

I do a lot of my writing while sitting in my local Starbucks coffee shop. The current manager, Liz, laughs a lot, and her cheerfulness seems to spread to her staff. I noticed it one morning in particular when she just exploded into laughter and two of the other girls behind the bar did the same. Liz's good cheer had spread to them. But it didn't stop there.

I noticed that I had developed a big smile on my face as I listened to the laughter. Then I looked around and several of the customers were also smiling, both in the queue and at the tables.

I was still thinking of laughter and smiling when I arrived home a few hours later. I was in an upbeat mood when I spoke to Elizabeth, and she seemed in better spirits afterwards. Her dad,

Peter, phoned shortly afterwards and they had a good laugh on the phone.

I am in no doubt that some of Liz's good cheer in Starbucks infected me, then Elizabeth and then her dad too – three degrees of separation. Liz has never met Peter, but she contributed to his laughter that day.

## CONTAGIOUS SMILING

Smiling is good for us. It reduces blood pressure and stress and produces serotonin, dopamine and endorphins in the brain – hormones which make us feel good. Scowling, on the other hand, can suppress the immune system and make us feel bad.[1]

When we smile at someone, even a stranger, they (almost) always smile back. Try it out as a simple experiment. Some people will think you're a little odd but, hey, that's their stuff.

Smiling is actually quite easy. It takes much less physical energy to smile than to frown. It only takes 17 facial muscles to smile but it takes 43 to frown. I'm all about saving energy.

Here's a new mathematical formula for you:

$$S = H^2$$

### (Smile = Happiness squared)

OK, it's really that smiling equals happiness *shared*, but it sounds the same as *squared* and might bring a smile to the face of the science and maths geeks reading this – like me.

We share happiness when we smile. We really do. When we smile in public, happiness leaves us and spreads like a virus, jumping from one person to the next. You can do a lot of good when you smile in public, and most of it you will never even know about.

And when you smile at someone, it takes an effort for them not to smile back at you. Returning a smile is an involuntary response.

In one experimental example of this, performed by scientists at Uppsala University in Sweden, 48 volunteers were asked to look at some pictures of happy, angry or neutral faces and smile, frown or be expressionless in return. The catch was that they weren't always to respond to a happy face with a smile or a sad face with a frown, but were sometimes told to do the opposite, to counter a happy face with a frown for instance, or not respond at all.

Their facial muscle movements were analysed by facial EMG and it was found that they didn't have complete control over them. When asked to frown at a happy face, their minds exerted some control over their muscles, but it took some effort. Their *zygomaticus major* muscles twitched automatically, indicating the birth of a smile. As the saying goes, 'A smile confuses an approaching frown.'

And when they were not supposed to react, facial EMG showed that they *did* react to the faces, with a smile for the happy face and a frown for the angry face.[2]

So even when someone doesn't smile back at you, you can pretty much guarantee that their smile muscles have twitched a bit.

Here's a poem about contagious smiling. I couldn't find the author as it's one of those things that go around the world several times on emails. I wanted to share it, though, because it might make you smile:

*Smiling is contagious,*

*You catch it like the 'flu.*

*When someone smiled at me today,*

*I started smiling too.*

*I passed around the corner,*

*And someone saw my grin,*

*When he smiled I realized*

*I'd passed it on to him!*

*I thought about that smile,*

*Then realized its worth:*

*A single smile – just like mine*

*Could travel round the Earth!*

*So, if you feel a smile begin,*

*Don't leave it undetected –*

*Let's start an epidemic quick*

*And get the world infected!*

Have you ever heard of a Duchenne smile? A Duchenne smile, or D-smile, is known as a genuine, authentic smile.[3] It was first identified in the mid-nineteenth century by French doctor Guillaume Duchenne while he was researching the physiology of facial expressions. You can recognize it because it produces little wrinkles at the sides of the eyes that look like crow's feet. It contracts the *orbicularis oculi*, the muscle that orbits the eyes, as well as the *zygomaticus major*.

A D-smile is associated with a genuine expression of joy. So if you could pass on a D-smile, you could spread joy everywhere you went without even saying a word. And D-smiles make a big difference to your own fortunes too.

A 2001 study performed by researchers at the University of California at Berkeley studied the expressions of 111 smiling women in their college yearbook. They followed up on the women 30 years later. Incredibly, the way they had smiled had a substantial bearing on their lives.

The women who had had a genuine Duchenne smile were more likely to be happily married and enjoy good well-being than those who hadn't, and this was even after the researchers controlled for physical attractiveness.[4]

## THREE DEGREES OF 'HAVE A NICE DAY!'

I spent a year as a chemistry lecturer from 2004 to 2005. I was writing my first book at the time and the income helped me to self-publish it.

One evening I was on the way to my once-a-week additional evening job teaching chemistry in the adult education department of Glasgow University. As usual I had taken the train to the city centre and was walking a little over a mile to the west end of the city.

I got thinking about an old friend of mine called Kim, who lived in Idaho in the US, and how his good cheer was always infectious. It was hard not to feel good when Kim was happy.

In particular, I recalled that every time we were in a café, restaurant or even bookshop, Kim would say, 'Have a nice day' to the waiter or shop assistant as we left. And he would say it with *purpose* – it wasn't just a random utterance that came out of his mouth. He would look each person in the eye and mean what he said. I remembered seeing a smile appear on people's faces as he wished them a nice day.

There was a small shop about halfway on my walk that I always stopped at to buy a snack prior to the three-hour class. So I decided to say 'Have a nice day' to the shop assistant, just as Kim would have done. I must admit that I felt a little odd, embarrassed almost. I was really much more of a 'Thanks' kind of person. But I did it anyway. And it felt quite good.

I decided to try it out a few more times in other places and gradually got over the embarrassment. It soon became a bit of a habit with me.

Then one evening, as I was entering the small shop on the way to the adult education class, I heard the assistant say 'Have a nice day' to a customer. And as I waited in the queue to be served, I realized he was saying it to every single customer. I couldn't help smiling. Kim's message had caught on. This was totally unexpected. I had only been saying it myself to spread some good cheer; it had never occurred to me that it might be contagious.

By the end of the university term, all of the assistants in that shop were saying 'Have a nice day' to all of the customers, at least as far as I could tell. 'A job well done,' I thought. I wondered how many people had been given service with a smile in that shop. It might even have improved the profits.

Elizabeth and I moved to Windsor the following year and I started wishing a nice day to every waiter and shop assistant who served me there. They seemed a little surprised at first. This clearly wasn't normal.

We regularly bought baguette sandwiches from a shop called EAT and I always said, 'Have a nice day' when I was leaving the service counter. Then one day, the man who was serving me said it to me first. I remember smiling to myself as I thought, 'He stole my line' – and *that* line I actually stole from Robin Williams in the excellent film *Good Will Hunting*. It's contagious!

As the weeks went by, a gradual contagion process took place in EAT as more and more of the staff started wishing customers a nice day.

Then, in a furniture shop, a man who sold us a desk wished me a nice day. A few days later I saw him buying his lunch in EAT. Coincidence? Maybe. But I'd like to think that he was a regular in EAT and caught the 'Have a nice day' bug from there.

There must now be several hundred people at least, maybe thousands, in Windsor who have been wished a nice day. Well done, Kim!

Obviously I can't really be certain that this had anything to do with me or Kim. I didn't exactly do a controlled study. But I'd like to think it did. And the reason I'm telling you this is so that you can try it out too. Go on, try it! It's a nice thing to do and makes people smile.

And try this experiment too: smile at people all day today. On purpose! Either it'll make them smile or it'll get them thinking. As the saying goes, 'Keep smiling. It makes people wonder what you've been up to.'

## FAKE IT 'TIL YOU MAKE IT

Do we smile because we are happy or are we happy because we smile? I think mostly we smile when we are happy or because we see someone else smiling or hear them laugh, but evidence also suggests that we can make ourselves happy by smiling.

According to the facial feedback hypothesis, facial movement can influence emotional experience.[5] The psychologist William James noticed this over 100 years ago and believed that bodily changes were required to feel emotion. And in *The Expression of Emotions in Man and Animals*, Darwin wrote, 'Even the simulation of an emotion tends to arouse it in our minds.'[6]

Try this simple exercise to test it for yourself. Pull a huge smile and allow yourself to move into a little chuckle if you want as you exhale. Now, while still smiling, try to feel sad. Can you do it? Your facial expressions and physiology are saying 'happy' and they generate the emotions. You can't have a body saying 'happy' and a mind saying 'sad'.

In 1992, psychologist Paul Ekman showed that when we smile or grimace, we experience changes in how we feel and throughout our autonomic nervous system. For instance, when volunteers were instructed to smile they felt happier, they felt less happy when they grimaced, and their heart rate and skin conductance changed depending upon whether they smiled or grimaced.[7]

Elizabeth tells me that when she has to do a crying scene, she really does feel very sad and it can take time to shake it off. The first time she had to cry on set was while filming a scene of the popular ITV drama *Trial and Retribution*, in which she played a homeless prostitute whose pimp had been murdered. Her first scene required her to cry while she explained to the police what had happened. In the scene she really did feel very upset. She was living the sadness of the character that she played, and the viewers were moved as a result.

To make herself cry, Elizabeth has to use her facial muscles to 'fake it', while at the same time she intensifies it by conjuring up a memory of a sad experience. She also prods her solar plexus because when emotionally traumatized you feel sick to the stomach, as a lot of emotion is held there. Then the tears flow automatically.

There is much powerful evidence now that our physiology 'feels' the emotion before we subjectively feel it.

In 2000, researchers at the University of Iowa College of Medicine asked 41 volunteers to conjure up a vivid memory of an emotional experience. This could be a happy or a sad memory or one charged with anger or fear, i.e. one of four primary emotions. They were asked to raise their hands to indicate the moment when they were actually feeling the emotion.

Intriguingly, heart rate and skin conductance – aspects of their autonomic nervous system – responded *before* they actually felt the emotion (before they raised their hands) and brain imaging showed that emotional areas became activated *when* they felt the emotion. As researchers wrote, '...the enactment of emotion precedes the feeling state.'[8]

Perhaps what happens is that the muscles used in the physical experience of an emotion send signals to the brain areas that correspond to that emotion and it is then that we get the actual emotional feeling. After that, of course, we can use our thoughts to alter the emotion if we wish, which can then feed back to the muscles, intensifying the new emotion.

We tend to think of emotion as the feelings we have, but evidence like this suggests that there's much more to it than that. An emotion may well be a combination of physiological, neural and subjective parts – the sum of the effect over the entire body and mind. In a sense, an emotion can be said to be smeared across the entire brain and body.

William James wrote, 'The bodily changes follow directly the perception of the exciting fact, and … our feeling of the same changes as they occur *is* the emotion.' He argued that we 'feel sorry because we cry, angry because we strike, afraid because we tremble, and not that we cry, strike, nor tremble because we are sorry, angry, or fearful, as the case may be'.[9]

His proposition – that the physiological changes come first – is the opposite way round from what most people assume – that the mental state comes first.

The idea that the mental state is due to the experience of the bodily changes is known as the 'James–Lange theory', after William James and Danish psychologist Carle Lange, who proposed the same thing at around the same time.[10] This theory is not as popular today among academics, who lean more towards the view that bodily states don't exactly initiate the mental state but in fact modulate it.

I propose that it's a bit of both. Physiology and facial expression can initiate an emotion and an emotion can initiate facial and physiological reactions. Which comes first? It depends upon the starting situation. Since emotion is 'smeared' throughout the brain and body in my opinion, then any starting point, whether it be a thought, a feeling or a bodily or facial movement, can initiate the feeling throughout the entire organism.

One 1998 study invited a group of volunteers to look at photographs of people either smiling or frowning. Another group was asked to copy the expressions and a third group was asked to copy the expressions while looking at themselves in a mirror.

The mood of those who simply looked at the photos didn't change, but those who copied the facial expressions did experience a change in mood. When they copied the positive expressions they felt more positive and when they copied the negative expressions they felt less positive. In this case, the facial expression initiated the emotion. It was the starting point.

Interestingly, those who copied the expressions while looking at themselves doing so in a mirror experienced even greater mood changes, feeling even more positive when they viewed themselves copying positive expressions, and even less positive when viewing themselves frowning.[11]

Smiling at yourself in the mirror, however silly it might feel initially, can go a long way to helping you to feel better.

## SMILING FOR HAPPINESS

So, smiling is contagious. When we see someone smile, our facial muscles automatically react, our body physiology takes on a positive tone, our brain fires in positive emotional regions and we feel happy.

If you're feeling low, could smiling actually help you to feel better? Many sceptics would think not, but evidence certainly suggests that you can fake it 'til you make it. It might take sustained effort, but it is possible.

One study found that smiling can be an effective treatment for depression, concluding that depressive states can lessen if you smile frequently.[12]

Of course, putting on a happy face doesn't work for everyone and will depend upon the degree of depression. It might even divert people from seeking effective treatment. The scenario where people pretend that everything is OK when they are around people but once they get home they burst into tears is actually known as 'smiling depression'.[13] Smiling has to be done on purpose, with intent, as an intervention. Rather than pretending everything's OK, it's best to acknowledge how you feel, but also show a willingness to keep smiling as a strategy to climb your way to a happier state.

These results explain why laughter therapy is a powerful therapy for people who are feeling sad or depressed. Patch Adams, the doctor well known for his portrayal in the Hollywood film that bears his name, literally laughed himself out of depression.

Ever heard the phrase 'go the extra mile'? Well, as Laugh Doctor Cliff Kuhn, MD, says, 'Always *go the extra smile*.' He has given that prescription to hundreds of depressed patients and reports that 'Those willing to practise it experience mood elevation and a reduction in symptoms – almost instantly.'[14] It's especially powerful if you're 'sick and tired of being sick and tired' and willing to give it a go.

If you are feeling depressed, practise smiling as often as you can. Say things with a smile. Smile at yourself several times every time you see yourself in a mirror. With practice it becomes easier and your facial muscles get used to it. Of course, this doesn't mean you shouldn't continue with any other treatment you may have been prescribed – it's something that you can do *as well*. Smile whenever the thought of smiling pops into your mind.

As the saying goes, 'If you don't start out the day with a smile, it's not too late to start practising for tomorrow.'

My friend Joe Hoare, a laughter teacher, taught me a simple yet powerful exercise: you take a deep breath in and let out a laugh on the out-breath. Practise it several times a day. It makes smiling and laughter much easier.

## CONTAGIOUS LAUGHTER

*'A laugh is a smile that bursts.'*[15]

Mary H. Waldrip

When I was at school, my English teacher once scolded one of my friends for laughing at the back of the class. His response was priceless: 'I wasn't laughing, I was just smiling loudly.'

There's a lot of similarity between smiling and laughter. A 2006 study by researchers at University College London and Imperial College London showed that laughter impacts the areas of the brain that are activated when we smile, which, when you think about it, makes sense. We smile when we laugh. But the key is that it's an automatic thing. It happens regardless of whether we're in on a joke we hear or even know what's funny. Have you ever tried to suppress laughter and then one person lets out a little squeak? You can't hold it in. The laughter itself is contagious.

In the study, 20 volunteers lay inside MRI scanners and listened to pleasant sounds like laughter or triumph (cheering) or unpleasant sounds like screaming or retching (fear and disgust). Each sound activated the mirror neurons for facial expressions and sound, since the brain was preparing the face to take on the appropriate facial expression and mimic the appropriate sounds. Interestingly, the activation was twice as high for laughter and cheers (high arousal emotions), which indicates that they might be more contagious than the negative sounds.[16]

I think just about everyone has caught themselves laughing if others are laughing. Just as with smiling, it takes an effort not to do so, even if we don't get the joke. The D-smiles of those laughing are contagious to us and our own smile muscles start to twitch. Before long, we burst into laughter ourselves.

And laughing is good for our health. It can be a bit like internal jogging, as it exercises the abdominal muscles. It's also good for the immune system. And, of course, it makes us feel happy.

Victor Hugo wrote, 'Laughter is the sun that drives winter from the human face.'[17]

And an Irish proverb goes, 'A good laugh and a long sleep are the best cures in the doctor's book.'

## A SMILE CAN MAKE YOU FEEL LIKE A MILLION DOLLARS

A 2005 study analysed smiles from a range of different people, from children, family, friends and loved ones to celebrities and even royalty. One hundred and nine volunteers looked at different photographs while having brain activity and electromagnetic heart activity measured. The brain and heart activity was compared to the activity when the people were given chocolate or money.

The researchers found that seeing a baby or child smiling was equivalent to eating 2,000 bars of chocolate or receiving £16,000 in cash. The smile of a loved one was also powerful, equating to about 600 chocolate bars or £8,500 in cash. A friend's smile was worth 200 chocolate bars or £145.

Dr David Lewis, a psychologist who analysed the results, commented, 'The powerful emotions triggered when someone important in our lives smiles at us and we smile back changes our brain chemistry.'[18]

So perhaps if we spend a whole morning smiling at people we might really feel like a million dollars.

## SERVICE WITH A SMILE

Japanese people are known to have relatively neutral facial expressions a lot of the time, but business leaders in Japan noticed that Japanese employees sold much more to westerners when they smiled. Now, some Japanese businesses conduct smile workshops where they put pencils or chopsticks in between employees' teeth to exercise their smile muscles. Just as lifting weights exercises your biceps, so holding a pen between your teeth exercises your *zygomaticus major* muscles, making smiling easier and more natural to you. And, of course, it stimulates the emotion of happiness.

One study actually found that if a person read a pleasant sentence with a pen between their teeth to create a smile, they read it faster than if they held the pen in their lips, which prevented a smile.[19] When we're smiling, we feel better and take in positive information much more effectively.

And the smile is passed around the workplace and beyond. As we know, this can have an impact upon company profits. People tend to want to be served by people who pass on good cheer, and whether they spend money with a particular company or not can have more to do with how the service makes them feel than with the actual price or quality of the product they buy.

Elizabeth's father, Peter, was the sales director of a large company for a number of years. He told me that one of the key things that made him so successful in his job was that his customers liked him. He built up very good relationships with them, and even when other companies came in with lower prices, he rarely lost business. One of his customers told him once that his company didn't buy from Peter's company, they bought from Peter. And that made all the difference!

Company profits depend a lot on customer satisfaction (we know this as the service-profit chain), but customer satisfaction itself can have a lot to do with attitudes and happiness within a corporation. So, as we have already seen, how an employee feels can have an impact upon company profits. And smiling staff can infect a lot of customers with good cheer, even down the phone line.

CHAPTER 14

# CAN YOU CATCH HAPPINESS?

**'But O, how bitter a thing it is to look into happiness through another man's eyes.'**

William Shakespeare

Think of happiness as being like a bug – one that doesn't make us sick but makes us smile. There really is such a thing. Happiness infects everyone that comes into contact with it. This is why we enjoy hanging out with cheerful people.

Using tools and techniques to increase our own happiness also works, as readers of positive psychology and self-help material know, but staggering new research shows that helping to raise the happiness of our friends might have as much of an effect.

## HAPPY FRIENDS MATTER

Using data from the Framingham Heart Study and statistical analysis, Fowler and Christakis calculated what would happen

181

to a person's happiness if one of their friends or other social ties (friends, family, neighbours, co-workers) flipped from being unhappy to happy during a given time period.

They measured happiness in a way typical of psychology studies, using part of the Center for Epidemiological Studies depression scale. On average, they found that the chances of anyone becoming happy increased by 15 per cent if an immediate social contact became happier. But this statistic hid the important find that the actual type and quality of relationship mattered.

For instance, just counting your friends, you have a 25 per cent chance of becoming happy if a friend becomes happy. With close (mutual) friends who live close to each other (within about a mile), if one becomes happy it increases the probability that the other will become happy by a whopping 63 per cent.[1] So, if a close friend of yours becomes happy soon there is a fairly high chance that you'll become happier too.

As we know from online social networking, 'friend' is a broad term. Most people only have a small number of close friends – between two and six. But if someone asked us to name our friends, we would list more people than this. We'd include people we see from time to time but we're not that close to.

It turns out that the spread of happiness depends upon the type of friend. Happiness is more contagious to us if we are close to a person, or if we like them. If I named William as a friend, for instance, whether he named me or not, his happiness would have a 25 per cent effect upon me. This is the 25 per cent figure quoted above. But if William named me as a friend and I didn't name him, the effect would only be 12 per cent. If we named each other, though, the effect of his happiness on my happiness would be 63 per cent.

The contagiousness of happiness is also greater within the sexes than between them. In other words, it transmits more between two women or two men than between a woman and a man.

Spouses who live together only have a weak effect upon each other's happiness. If one becomes happy, the probability of the other becoming happy is only 8 per cent, although, like all of these statistics, it is an average over thousands of people. For some couples the effect will be greater than for others.

Significantly, a next-door neighbour has more of an effect on happiness than a spouse. The chance of you becoming happy if your next-door neighbour does is 34 per cent, though again this will vary from person to person and depends on how much contact you actually have with your neighbours. Framingham, Massachusetts, where the data came from for the study, is a small town, and small towns tend to have closer ties between neighbours. So the likelihood won't be the same in cities or with people who don't see their neighbours much. The neighbour effect can be high, though. Some people like their neighbours a lot and look on them as close friends and confidants. They see a lot of them and so soak up their positive emotions. Neighbours don't have the same effect with depression, however, because depression causes us to withdraw from people.

Brothers and sisters who live close to each other (within a mile) have a 14 per cent effect upon each other. They are not as influential as friends. Most people spend more time with friends than they do with family.

## THE EFFECT OF PHYSICAL DISTANCE

The contagiousness of happiness depends in part on how much time you spend with people. This in turn can depend on how far apart you live. Friends who live close by impact you more than those who live farther away because you tend to see them more. But for those who live even closer – less than half a mile – you have a 42 per cent chance of becoming happy if they do (25 per cent for up to a mile). But as geographical closeness tails off, so also does the chance of a friend's happiness making you happy. If they live up to two miles away, the probability drops to 22 per cent. For up to three miles it falls to 10 per cent and is then 8 per cent for distances of up to ten miles away.

What this shows us is that living in a small community might be better for happiness than living in a less densely connected one. It also shows us that how our friends feel really matters in terms of our own happiness. And that their happiness, in part, depends upon our happiness.

## ALL IN GOOD TIME

The impact of a friend on your happiness depends upon *when* that friend became happy. The greatest impact a friend (living less than half a mile from you) can have, 42 per cent, is if they became happy within the past six months, but the effect is still strong (35 per cent) for up to a year.

So, just as the contagiousness of happiness decreases with distance, so it also decreases with time. As we move further away in space or time from the focal point, the source of an outbreak of happiness, the strength of the effect gradually reduces.

When something changes in our lives we eventually get used to it and it's no longer a big deal. What might be happening with happiness is that a friend gets used to their new-found happiness and we get used to them being happy so that it no longer has the same impact upon us.

## WHAT ABOUT THIRD FACTORS?

Just as with the analysis of depression, in the Fowler and Christakis study there were clear clusters of happy people. It's almost certainly true that happy people make friends with other happy people, just as people befriend people with similar interests. This is called homophily. But Fowler and Christakis accounted for homophily in their research by following the changes in happiness over time and their analysis showed that happiness in one person actually caused happiness in another.

Could something have happened to make a whole group of people happy at the same time, like a new cinema or theatre opening in the town? The researchers accounted for this too by taking the direction of friendships into account. If a new cinema had come to town and been the cause of a cluster of happy people, it would have affected one-sided friendships just as much as close (mutual) friends, just as the sun shines equally on everyone.

There is a little debate in the scientific journals about the actual strength of the effect, but the bottom line is that happiness *is* contagious. It spreads from person to person.

## CENTRE OR OUTSIDE?

As we have already seen, happy people tend to have more friends and social contacts and therefore be closer to the centre of their networks. They are more connected. Unhappy people, on the contrary, tend to be on the peripheries of their networks and to have fewer friends or social connections.

There is no doubt that your position in a social network affects your happiness. It is affecting you right now. If you want to be happy, get connected.

Think of it another way: the more people the people you are connected to are connected to, the greater your chance of becoming happier in the future. If you become friends with someone with a lot of connections you will have moved closer to the centre of the social network and will become happier as a result.

We need social connections. We need to bond with each other. The human brain, heart and nervous system require it, as we learned from the research on infants earlier.

The Fowler and Christakis study found that an increase in centrality in a social network from low to medium centrality or from medium to high centrality (two standard deviations) increased the probability of happiness by 14 per cent, where centrality was a measure of not only how connected you are but how well connected are the people that you are connected to.

So, if you become friends with a popular person there's a fairly good chance that you will become happier over the next year.

One way to tackle unhappiness, then, is by first looking at how connected you are. Therapists could do this for their clients and then make some suggestions for becoming more connected, maybe joining a group, taking an evening class or attending a dance class – something that will be likely to have a fair few happy people there. Each friendly connection a person makes raises the chance of improvements in their happiness.

What if a sad person moves into our community? Do we ignore them for fear of their effect on the network? But the moment they interact with someone they are connected. They are part of the network. Ignoring them is detrimental to everyone, as we learned earlier. If we help them to fit in, on the other hand, the entire community benefits.

Be there for people in need. Enter their presence with full awareness of contagion and you will be immune to any sadness. You will recognize that any feelings of unhappiness are not your own and compassion will replace them. And, with this awareness, *your* mood will be the one that's transmitting. Happiness is stronger than unhappiness. At least that's what the study showed.

Using statistical analysis, the researchers found that each person who was happy increased the probability that a person they were connected to socially would be happy by 9 per cent. But each unhappy person decreased the probability of happiness by 7 per cent.[2]

Friendship, it seems, is an antidote to unhappiness. One of my all-time favourite quotes relates to its importance. It comes from Khalil Gibran:

*'In the sweetness of friendship, let there be laughter and sharing of pleasures. For in the dew of little things, the heart finds its morning and is refreshed.'*[3]

## THREE DEGREES OF SEPARATION

In terms of its impact on happiness, social distance follows the same pattern as distance in space and time. Remember that social distance is how many degrees of separation someone is from you? It turns out that happiness is contagious to three degrees of separation. In other words, the mother of your best friend's next-door neighbour can cause you to be happy and you can cause her to be happy, even if you never meet her in your lifetime.

The average effect of all types of social contact on happiness at one degree of separation was found to be 15 per cent, but incredibly it was still 10 per cent at two degrees of separation and astonishingly the probability of someone at three degrees of separation impacting a person's happiness was found to be 6 per cent.[4]

Let's put this into perspective. Let's assume you have 10 friends, and each of your friends also has 10 friends, and each of theirs also has 10 friends. In other words, you are connected to 1,000 people by three degrees of separation.

Since the chances of you impacting someone at three degrees of separation is 6 per cent, this means that you are impacting at least 60 people (6 per cent of 1,000). Isn't that fascinating? And you wondered how important or influential you were!

If you were to become happier for any reason, chances are you would be making at least 60 other people happier, most of whom you don't know or will ever know. One person's happiness influences the entire structure of a social network.

So something that we must now consider is that happiness is not just a product of *our* attitude, life experiences or genes. It is also strongly related to how those around us feel. If you want to be happier, either working on your own happiness or helping others to be happy will work, because any change in any person's happiness has a knock-on effect, and the net effect can be a gain for everyone.

You want the world to be a happier place? The buck stops with each of us.

## GET CONNECTED AND YOU MIGHT LIVE TO 100

Having a rich network of connections also increases your chances of living to 100. A 2010 study that examined 188 Australian people over 100 years of age showed that having a close network of family and friends was one of the key factors that determined their longevity.[5]

Genetics only accounts for about 20–30 per cent of the chances of living to 100. The rest is down to what you do, what you eat, how much exercise you take, your typical lifestyle and your attitude, and we must now add how connected you are to the equation.

For some, those connections can even be made while living in a nursing home. The researchers reported that even if a person didn't have a rich family network or didn't have children, '...if they have very strong connections with their friends or if they are living in a nursing home that gets them doing interesting things with others who live there, they are more likely to live to 100.'[6]

## WIDER CONNECTIONS

There's a parallel with biodiversity. The health of our planet is linked to the diversity of species. All species are connected to each other by virtue of the fact that the actions of one may benefit or hinder another and one might become food for another.

The greater the number of species (the denser the ecological net), the healthier the planet. Making extinct too many species can spell ecological disaster. Similarly, a diverse array of friends and social connections is linked with the health of our minds and hearts. When we reduce the number of these connections (make extinct too many social ties), we reduce the health of our minds and hearts.

There's a parallel too with the density of connections in the human neural net. A richly connected prefrontal cortex is linked with emotional well-being, self-control and happiness. A less dense neural net is linked with depression, emotional instability, lack of self-control and unhappiness.

Even at a cosmic level, a galaxy with a greater density of stars, planets, comets and asteroids offers a greater chance for life to spread.

It seems that at the heart of all things, being connected sustains life.

Perhaps the roots of connecting go right to the core of reality. We know that at an elementary level, subatomic particles strive to connect. It is the connecting of these particles, facilitated by the four known forces of nature, that produces all matter in the universe.

Quite simply, connecting is what life does, and it is through our own connections that our emotions, attitudes and behaviour are transmitted. Perhaps there is no other reason for us to be here than to form bonds with each other, for in the process of connecting, life flows through us.

Perhaps we are conduits for life. I am reminded of the words of the philosopher and humanitarian Albert Schweitzer, 'True philosophy must start from the most immediate and comprehensive fact of consciousness: "I am life that wants to live, in the midst of life that wants to live."'[7]

What aspect of life could be driving the connectedness? Perhaps we can only begin to understand this through the process of connecting itself. It could be love. For in the depths of the bonds we form, love blossoms like a seed sown in fertile ground.

Perhaps, then, to love is the purpose of life.

# CHAPTER 15

# IS KINDNESS CONTAGIOUS?

**'Kindness can become its own motive. We are made kind by being kind.'**
Eric Hoffer

We've seen how children can pick up aggression and violence from video games and from TV, but is kindness contagious in this way too?

In my last book, *Why Kindness Is Good for You*, I looked at a simple study in which children watched a Lassie movie. Readers may remember the movies of the 1970s where Lassie the dog frequently showed great courage and compassion as she rescued humans from danger.

There were two groups of children in the study. One saw a part of the movie that contained a scene of Lassie's owner rescuing Lassie's puppies. But for another group of children that scene was deleted. The question was, would that affect the children's behaviour?

Later, the children were playing a game that was interrupted by sounds of distressed puppies. Going to help would mean losing points, but more of the children who had seen the rescuing scene went to help more quickly than those who hadn't.[1]

In another study of the contagiousness of kindness, children watched a video of a bowling competition where the winner gave his winning certificate to charity. Other children were also shown the video but not that last part. Later, when all the children were given certificates themselves, those who had seen the donation scene were more likely to give theirs away than those who hadn't seen it.[2]

## THE MOTHER TERESA EFFECT

Mother Teresa won the 1979 Nobel Peace Prize. She dedicated her life to caring for the sick, poor and hungry, and became a world symbol of kindness and compassion.

In another study I outlined in my last book, 132 students at Harvard University watched her carrying out acts of kindness in a 50-minute video. Swabs of saliva were taken from them before and immediately afterwards to measure a component of the immune system known as salivary immunoglobulin A. The levels had risen by the time the film had finished and incredibly were still elevated one hour later. The scientists suggested that this might have been because the students '...continued to dwell on the loving relationships that characterized the film.'[3]

Isn't it true that we run inspirational things over and over in our minds afterwards?

And the strength of Mother Teresa's kindness shows that one person really can change the world.

## ONE KIND ACT INSPIRES ANOTHER

Think of when someone does something kind for you, even something as simple as holding a door open for you. Don't you feel yourself wanting to do the same for another?

Acts of kindness travel through our social networks, rippling outwards like waves from a pebble dropped in a pond. We have all seen this kind of thing in our own lives and it has now even been examined in a controlled laboratory setting.

In a 2010 study at the University of California, San Diego, and Harvard University participants played a type of game called a 'public goods game', a game used in experimental economics. In the game, groups of people are given tokens equivalent to money and have to choose how many they want to place into a public pot and how many they want to keep. If they're given 20 tokens, for example, they might choose to place 8 into the public pot and keep 12 for themselves. Then all the tokens in the group's pot are split evenly. If everyone put their whole 20 tokens into the public pot, when it was split they would end up with 20 tokens again. But someone could choose to only contribute a small number of tokens and if their other team mates put more in the public pot, then they would end up with more than the 20 tokens they started with and their team mates would have fewer than 20.

Several rounds of the game were played, with the groups changing each time, and the researchers worked out the effect of players' behaviour on one another in subsequent rounds. They noted, for instance, if one person made a large contribution to the public good, and what effect, if any, it had on others in the next couple of rounds.

Indeed, it did have an effect. When a person made a large contribution to the public good, others in that group, who were then in different groups for the next rounds, made large contributions in those rounds. And it didn't stop there. Players in those groups were similarly affected and contributed more in later rounds. The effect of each act spread outwards to three degrees of separation.

And one act didn't just affect the acts of one other person but of several. If changing the world means causing others to show more kindness, then this simple experiment demonstrates that one person really can have an impact.

The researchers concluded, '…as a result, each person in a network can influence dozens or even hundreds of people, some of whom he or she does not know and has not met.'[4]

An act of kindness is *never* a stand-alone act. Each ripples outwards from its source, touching hearts and minds even in far-flung places.

## A MIRROR OF KINDNESS

Earlier we learned that people like us more when we mimic them, regardless of whether we do it unconsciously or on purpose. We all mimic people unconsciously in fact, as our mirror neurons fire in response to what we see on their faces and in their body language.

People who are more empathetic mimic more. Empathy is an expression of connectedness and a form of kindness. So it's interesting that research now shows that mimicking others actually makes them kinder.

In one such study, an experimenter conducted a fake marketing survey with 17 volunteers, one at a time. Each volunteer had to verbally state their opinion about specific advertisements. While they were doing so, the experimenter mimicked the posture and arm and leg movements of half of them.

The experimenter then said that she had to leave the room briefly to collect some stuff for a second experiment and returned after about 30 seconds. When she passed the participant she 'accidentally' dropped six pens. The aim of the experiment was to see if the participant would help her pick them up and how long it would take them to act.

All of the participants who had been mimicked picked up the pens but only one third of those who hadn't been mimicked did so.[5]

A mood questionnaire also showed that the participants who had been mimicked felt better. They did not know why. They had no idea that they had been mimicked.

Kindness makes us feel connected. And it's a two-way street. Empathy promotes kindness and kindness promotes empathy because it reduces the emotional distance between people. We mimic more, then, when we're kind, and, as the study showed, mimicking encourages kindness, and so it goes on. Kindness is contagious.

In a second experiment, the fake survey was done again with a different (larger) group of participants, but with one crucial difference. After leaving the room, a different experimenter entered (to run the next part of the supposed experiment) and dropped her pens. The results were similar to the first part of the study: 84 per cent of those who had been mimicked helped her pick them up but only 48 per cent of those who hadn't been mimicked did so.[6]

In other words, the kindness extended to two degrees of separation.

In a third part of the experiment, after the fake survey the experimenter explained to each participant that the task was over, they would soon start on the next task and that they would now be paid for their participation (each person was to receive two euros). She then gave them four 50 cent coins.

Before she left the room, the experimenter also told the participant about a charity (CliniClowns, a Dutch charity that tries to alleviate the suffering of seriously ill children in hospital) that the university was supporting, asked them to fill out a form with some questions about the charity and said that they were free to donate some money if they wanted to by dropping it in a white box. It was clear to the participant that the forms and donations would be completely anonymous.

Again the results were similar: 76 per cent of those who had been mimicked donated money, while only 43 per cent of those who hadn't been mimicked donated. And those who had been mimicked actually donated double the amount of money: almost 80 cents compared with 40 cents for those who hadn't been mimicked.[7]

## ABSORBING LOVE FROM THE ENVIRONMENT

Our home environment is usually a reflection of ourselves. A figure or a painting of a couple holding hands, for instance, would not be out of place in the home of a couple with a strong loving relationship. In a way, their love spreads to the décor of their home. Research now suggests that it can even be transferred from the décor to the children.

This was shown by an experiment involving 60 18-month-old children. They were divided into groups and shown photographs of typical household objects (e.g. a teapot) but the key to the experiment was that each photograph contained something in the background to prime the children. In one set of pictures there were two wooden dolls standing very close together and facing one another (the 'together' condition). In another there was just a single doll (the 'alone' condition). A third had two dolls with their backs to each other and a fourth was a neutral stack of coloured blocks.

The experiment started up with a brief game of chase involving the children, the experimenter and an assistant. Then the assistant showed the children the photographs. After that the assistant told them to play with the experimenter, at which point the experimenter left the room and returned with a bundle of six small sticks, which she 'accidentally' dropped.

The purpose of the study was to see how long it would take the children to help her pick them up and whether this had any bearing on the photographs that they had been shown.

Sixty percent of the children who had seen the 'together' photographs (nine children) spontaneously helped. Yet only 20 per cent (three children) in each of the other groups helped.[8]

What does this mean? It means that infants' kindness can be influenced easily by adults simply by adjusting things in the home.

Studies of this sort show that a child can absorb some of the parents' love from the home environment too. In this way, the parents' love for each other spreads outwards, touching their children, who then touch the lives of others.

And I'm sure you know by now that it won't just stop there, at two degrees of separation. Think of how many lives are touched when two people show their love for each other with a simple embrace, or a soft touch to the arm.

## INTERDEPENDENCE AND KINDNESS

As we have seen, mimicry builds rapport. In fact it's a classical strategy to 'win friends and influence people', but these last few experiments show us that mimicry, or priming, actually has kindness contagion effects.

When we imitate others, as we have seen, it makes them feel more connected to us and others. Studies have shown that being mimicked actually shifts a person's self-construal towards interdependence. Imitation 'heightens one's perception of interpersonal closeness'.[9]

The causal link between self-construal and kindness has also been demonstrated experimentally.[10]

In the first of a series of experiments, participants carried out a task while being subtly mimicked or not, then completed a self-construal test. Those who had been mimicked showed a greater amount of interdependent self-construal. In particular, women showed more than men.

In a second test, this interdependent self-construal was shown to apply to the participants' sense of connection with others. And again, women felt closer to people than men.

In a third experiment, after being mimicked, each participant was involved in a fake task which involved answering questions about travelling behaviour. The experimenter then told them that they would shortly be taking part in a second task with a different experimenter and escorted them to a waiting room.

Five chairs were placed in a row against the wall in the waiting room and a bag, jacket and some documents were lying on the chair furthest to the left, indicating that someone was occupying it. The participant then took a seat on one of the chairs. The key to the experiment was, which chair would they sit on?

It turned out that the people who had been mimicked sat closer to the occupied chair than those who hadn't been mimicked.

In a fourth experiment volunteers once again participated in an irrelevant task before filling out an interdependence/independence questionnaire. Their answers were coded for interdependence or independence by counting the number of times they said things like 'I am a sister' or 'I am a team captain' (interdependent) or 'I am intelligent' or 'I am athletic' (independent). Those who had been mimicked showed a greater interdependent self-construal.

With all studies of this type, participants are paid a small amount of money for their efforts at the end. This time, after being paid, the participants were asked if they would help a PhD student with his experiments by filling out an 'extended' version of a questionnaire. The only thing was that he had no research funding, so couldn't pay them. Would they help or not?

Seventy-two per cent of those who had been mimicked helped the student but only 38 per cent of those who hadn't been mimicked did so. And the volunteers who had shown the greatest interdependent self-construal were also the ones most likely to help the PhD student.

This series of experiments showed that interdependence is the factor that links mimicry with kindness.

So kindness, which promotes interdependence, ultimately promotes more kindness. And it spreads by causing us to feel connected to others.

# CHAPTER 16

# SINGLE ACTS CAN MAKE A BIG DIFFERENCE

**'When I was young, I admired clever people. Now that I am old, I admire kind people.'**

Abraham Joshua Heschel

People sometimes perform extraordinarily selfless acts of kindness, and these acts can go a long way, far beyond the original recipient, leaving a lasting impression on families, communities and even the world at large.

## THE DOMINO EFFECT OF KIDNEY DONATIONS

People who need kidney transplants often have family members who want to donate a kidney to them but are not a match. Still they co-register as a donor and, once their loved one receives a kidney, pledge to donate a kidney to someone they are a match for.

This sets off a 'donor chain' that resembles the concept of 'pay it forward'. One donation sets off another, which sets off another, which sets off another, and so on.[1] A single act of kindness by an altruistic donor can result in multiple organ donations spanning the length and breadth of the country, bringing families together and saving lives.

This is exactly what happened over a period of eight months when a single donor – a 28-year-old man from Michigan – donated a kidney to a woman in Phoenix, Arizona, on 18 July 2007 (no. 1). The woman's husband had been a willing donor but was not a match for his wife. However, eight days after she had received a kidney, he travelled to Toledo, Ohio, and donated one of his kidneys to a 32-year-old woman (no. 2). The woman's mother had wanted to donate a kidney to her but was also not a match. So she then travelled to Columbus two months later and donated one of her kidneys (on 13 September 2007) to a person at Ohio State University (no. 3). That person's co-registered donor then donated one of their kidneys to a man at the same hospital (no. 4). That man's sister then donated her kidney to a patient at Johns Hopkins Hospital (12 February 2008) (no. 5). That person's co-registered donor then donated one of their kidneys to a woman patient also at Johns Hopkins Hospital (no. 6). Her co-registered donor then donated a kidney to another patient at Johns Hopkins Hospital (no. 7), whose co-registered donor then donated one to a patient at Wake Forest University in North Carolina (no. 8). That patient's co-registered kidney was then donated to a patient back at Johns Hopkins Hospital (18 March 2008) (no. 9), whose co-registered donor donated a kidney to a 60-year-old woman in Toledo, Ohio (no. 10).[2]

The 28-year-old man probably has no idea that his kind act not only saved the life of the recipient of his kidney but actually initiated a series of events that saved the lives of another nine people.

## THE BASKET BRIGADE

History is filled with inspirational stories where one person has made a huge difference.

The inspirational coach Tony Robbins remembers when he was 11 years old and his family had no money and no food at Thanksgiving. Tony recounts, 'Then a miracle happened.'[3] There was a knock on the door. Tony's parents were arguing at the time on account of their desperate situation, so, being the eldest child, Tony answered it, only to be faced with a large man holding a box of food with a bag at his side containing an uncooked turkey.

The turkey and the box of food were for Tony and his family. The man, knowing that they were poor, was making them a gift at Thanksgiving – a selfless act of kindness!

'If strangers care about me and my family,' Tony thought, 'I'm going to care about strangers.' He promised himself, 'Someday I'd do well enough to do this for other families.'

He made his first gift of a basket of food when he was 17 years old. He didn't wait until he was wealthy. He bought food and filled two baskets for two families. Then he went to the local church, explained what he was doing and they recommended two families who were in need.

Tony dressed like a delivery boy to deliver the food and wrote a note to accompany each basket instead of telling them that he was the one who was providing it. His father had got upset when the man had arrived at the door when Tony was a child and he didn't want these people to get upset.

His note said, 'This is a gift from a friend. Please know that you're loved. I want you to have an extraordinary Thanksgiving. You deserve it. Please accept this gift.' Then underneath he wrote, 'If you can, someday do well enough to do this for one other family, and pass on the gift.' He signed off with, 'Love, a friend.'

He describes his first delivery. A Latino woman answered the door. She had five children and Tony later learned that her husband had left her three days earlier with no money or food. She let out a huge scream of joy, hugged and kissed Tony, who at that moment was trying to pretend that he was just the delivery boy. Then she sobbed, looking at Tony and crying, 'Gift from God!'

When he brought the food into the house, the children were ecstatic. And as he drove away he could see in his rear-view mirror that the woman was crying on the porch with her children, but with an enormous smile on her face. Seeing this, he pulled over and started sobbing uncontrollably.

It was a life-changing experience for him. He fed four families the following year, and eight the year after that. And he did it anonymously, without telling any of his family or friends what he was doing. Now, over three decades later, the 'Anthony Robbins International Basket Brigade' feeds people in dozens of countries around the world. An act of kindness at Tony's front door when he was an 11-year-old child changed his life forever, setting off a chain of kind acts that have inspired people all over the world to start basket brigades. Now, the movement feeds over two million people every year at Thanksgiving and Christmas, touching many, many lives along the way. And it is growing.

The guiding principle of the Basket Brigade is that 'One small act of generosity on the part of one caring person can transform the lives of hundreds.'

# CIVIL RIGHTS

Many will be familiar with the story of Rosa Parks. It began on 1 December 1955 in Montgomery, Alabama. She was secretary of the National Association for the Advancement of Coloured People (NAACP)[4] at the time and was on her way home from work. She took up a seat in the area of the bus reserved for white people and was asked to move but refused.

Rosa was arrested for her 'offence' and ended up in court. But this sparked outrage among black people, which resulted in a 381-day wave of bus boycotts that almost crippled Montgomery Buses. During that time, many African Americans walked for several miles each day just to get to work and back, rather than give their fares to the bus company.

By standing up for what she believed in, Rosa poured fuel on the civil rights movement, which grew to become a massive wave. Almost a year after her arrest, the US Supreme Court ruled that segregation on transportation was unconstitutional.

The civil rights movement also saw the emergence of Martin Luther King, whose non-violent methods were inspired by the teachings of Mahatma Gandhi. Shortly after Rosa Parks' arrest, on the evening of 5 December 1955, King gave a speech at Holt Street Baptist Church in Montgomery. In reference to the bus boycott, he said:

*'Right here in Montgomery, when the history books are written in the future, somebody will have to say, "There lived a race of people, a black people, 'fleecy locks and black complexion', but a people who had the moral courage to stand up for their rights. And thereby they injected a new meaning into the veins of history and of civilization."'*[5]

THE CONTAGIOUS POWER OF THINKING

With every speech King made, a new burst of contagion started as his words sparked a great passion in black people all over the country for personal freedom and the right to be treated equally. In his famous, 'I Have a Dream' speech, given on 28 August 1963 at an address on a march on Washington, DC, he closed with the also immortalized words:

> 'When we let freedom ring, when we let it ring from every village and every hamlet, from every state and every city, we will be able to speed up that day when all of God's children, black men and white men, Jews and Gentiles, Protestants and Catholics, will be able to join hands and sing in the words of the old Negro spiritual, "Free at last! Free at last! Thank God Almighty, we are free at last!"'[6]

And it did ring from every village and every hamlet, from every state and every city. It rang in the hearts and minds of black people throughout the nation, adding power to the wave that eventually culminated in the civil rights act of 1964 and the right to vote, and a black president on 20 January 2009.

The NAACP itself had actually begun with a group of 29 people led by W. E. B. Du Bois, the first African American to earn a PhD at Harvard University, and William Monroe Trotter, the first African American to be awarded a Phi Beta Kappa key at Harvard University. They had their first meeting in 1905 to discuss the challenges faced by 'people of colour' and what could be done about it. The meeting was held in Fort Erie, on the Canadian side of the Niagara River, and thus the group became known as the Niagara Movement.[7]

The initial meeting gave birth to the idea of the NAACP and many people were members of both, but the Niagara Movement disbanded a few years later and many of the members then joined the NAACP.

You could say that W. E. B. Du Bois, William Monroe Trotter and this initial group of 29 people literally sowed the seeds that changed the world. Their sense of fairness and justice, their passion for the rights of African Americans and their willingness to challenge the poor treatment of black people gradually spread across the continent.

Of course, earlier seeds will have been sown in each of these people's lives too. We can literally go back and back, but the point is that it only takes a small group of people to change the world. Others are then inspired and find the strength to stand up for what they believe in.

As the spiritual leader Billy Graham said, 'Courage is contagious. When a brave man takes a stand, the spines of others are often stiffened.'[8]

Little did Rosa Parks know that her actions would have such consequences. But the number 2857 bus that she refused to give up her seat on is famous. It's a GM 'old look' transit bus, with the serial number 1132, and is permanently housed at the Henry Ford Museum. Thousands who now step onto that bus are inspired. They *feel* Rosa Parks' power and determination, and it ignites inside many of them the will to create a better world, a fairer world for all.

✳✳✳✳✳

You too are contagious, regardless of whether you think you are or not. The question is, what do you want to spread?

The moment you make that choice, you change the future. Maybe a decision you make right now will change the course of history.

If you want to see a better world, be an example of better behaviour. If you want to see more kindness in your community, be an example to others in your community. If you want to see more peace, be an example of how to act without aggression. As Gandhi said, we must be the change we wish to see in the world.

Gandhi also achieved all that he did peacefully. Let his spirit be a guiding light to you. You need never be unkind in the pursuit of your dreams. On the contrary, acting with kindness in all of your encounters will make the consequences of your journey through this life all the more fulfilling for the extended family with whom you share this planet.

So hold your head high and know that you make a difference every time you smile at someone. A smile at a stranger can lift the spirits of hundreds of people you'll never know. Smile on purpose then, and mean it. And if that's all you do today, you've already made a difference.

There are people who feel that they don't matter in this world. We all do. We are all interconnected. Our thoughts and emotions are contagious. And every act has consequences.

So be warm. Be gentle. And be kind. As Mother Teresa said, 'Spread love everywhere you go. Let no one ever come to you without leaving happier.'[9]

# REFERENCES

## INTRODUCTION

1. J. N. Rosenquist, J. H. Fowler and N. A. Christakis, 'Social network determinants of depression', *Molecular Psychiatry*, 2010, 1–9

2. J. H. Fowler and N. A. Christakis, 'Dynamic spread of happiness in a large social network: longitudinal analysis over 20 years in the Framingham Heart Study', *British Medical Journal*, 2008, 337, a2,338, 1–9

3. N. A. Christakis and J. H. Fowler, 'The spread of obesity in a large social network over 32 years', *The New England Journal of Medicine*, 2007, 357(4), 370–79

4. R. G. Netemeyer, J. G. Maxham and D. R. Lichenstein, 'Store manager performance and satisfaction: effects on store employee performance and satisfaction, store customer satisfaction, and store customer spending growth', *Journal of Applied Psychology*, 2010, 95(3), 530–45

5. T. Moll, G. Jordet and G. J. Pepping, 'Emotional contagion in soccer penalty shootouts: celebration of individual success is associated with ultimate team success', *Journal of Sports Science*, 2010, 28(9), 983–92

## *CHAPTER 1:* 'I FEEL IT FROM YOUR FACE'

1. For a general review of mirror neurons, visit http://en.wikipedia.org/wiki/Mirror_neuron (last accessed on 21 January 2011). *See also* M. Iacoboni, *Mirroring People*,

Farrar, Straus, and Giroux, New York, 2008, *and* S. P. Tipper, 'From observation to action simulation: the role of attention, eye-gaze, emotion, and body state', *Quarterly Journal of Experimental Psychology*, 2010, 63(11), 2,081–105

2. R. Mukamel, A. D. Ekstrom, J. Kaplan, M. Iacoboni and I. Fried, 'Single neuron responses in humans during execution and observation of actions', *Current Biology*, 2010, 20(8), 750–56

3. C. A. Porro, P. Facchin, S. Fusi, G. Dri and L. Fadiga, 'Enhancement of force after action observation: behavioural and neurophysiological studies', *Neuropsychologia*, 2007, 45, 3,114–21

4. D. Ertelt, S. Small, A. Sodolkin, C. Dettmers, A. McNamara, F. Binkofski and G. Buccino, 'Action observation has a positive effect on rehabilitation of motor deficits after stroke', *Neuroimage*, 2007, 36(supplement 2), T164–73

5. L. H. P. Eggermont, D. F. Swaab, E. M. Hol and E. J. A. Scherder, 'Observation of hand movements by older persons with dementia: effects on cognition', *Dementia and Geriatric Cognitive Disorders*, 2009, 27, 366–74

6. H. S. Friedman and R. E. Riggio, 'Effect of individual differences in nonverbal expressiveness on transmission of emotion', *Journal of Nonverbal Behavior*, 1981, 6, 96–101

7. T. L. Chatrand and J. A. Bargh, 'The chameleon effect: the perception–behaviour link and social interaction', *Journal of Personality and Social Psychology*, 1999, 76(6), 893–910

8. M. Stel, R. B. van Baaren, J. Blascovich, E. van Dijk, C. McCall, M. M. Pollmann, M. L. van Leeuwen, J. Mastop and R. Vonk, 'Effects of *a priori* liking on the elicitation of mimicry', *Experimental Psychology*, 2010, 57(6), 412–18

9. A. G. Greenwald, D. E. McGhee and J. L. K. Schwartz, 'Measuring individual differences in implicit cognition: the implicit association test', *Journal of Personality and Social Psychology*, 1998, 74(6), 1,464–80. *See also* R. van Baaren, L. Janssen, T. L. Chatrand and A. Dijksterhuis, 'Where is the love? The social aspects of mimicry', *Philosophical Transactions of the Royal Society B*, 2009, 364(1,528), 2,381–9

10. L. Johnston, 'Behavioural mimicry and stigmatization', *Social Cognition*, 2002, 20(1), 18–35

11. Chatrand and Bargh, op. cit. *See also* van Baaren, Janssen, Chatrand and Dijksterhuis, op. cit.

12. J. N. Bailenson and N. Yee, 'Digital chameleons: automatic assimilation of nonverbal gestures in immersive virtual environments', *Psychological Science*, 2005, 16(10), 814–19

13. R. B. van Baaren, R. W. Holland, B. Steenaert and A. van Knippenberg, 'Mimicry for money: behavioural consequences of imitation', *Journal of Experimental Social Psychology*, 2003, 39, 393–8

14. Ibid. The study is described in this paper and was conducted by the same authors

15. U. Dimberg, M. Thunberg and K. Elmehed, 'Unconscious facial reactions to emotional facial expressions', *Psychological Science*, 2000, 11(1), 86–9

16. C. van der Gaag, R. B. Minderaa and C. Keysers, 'Facial expressions: what the mirror neuron system can and cannot tell us', *Social Neuroscience*, 2007, 2(3–4), 179–222

17. B. Wicker, C. Keysers, J. Plailly, J-P. Royet, V. Gallese and G. Rizolatti, 'Both of us disgusted in *my* insula: the common

neural basis of seeing and feeling disgust', *Neuron*, 2003, 40, 655–64

18. C. Keysers, B. Wicker, V. Gazzola, J-L. Anton, L. Fogassi and V. Gallese, 'A touching sight: SII/PV activation during the observation and experience of touch', *Neuron*, 2004, 42, 335–46

19. For a review of some of the research on the mirror neuron system, including how it works with emotions and empathy, *see* J. A. C. J. Bastiaansen, M. Thioux and C. Keysers, 'Evidence for mirror systems in emotions', *Philosophical Transactions of the Royal Society B*, 2009, 364,2,391–404

20. P. L. Jackson, A. N. Meltzoff and J. Decety, 'How do we perceive the pain of others? A window into the neural processes involved in empathy', *Neuroimage*, 2005, 24, 771–9

21. Y. Cheng, C-P. Lin, H-L. Liu, Y-H. Hsu, K-E. Lim, D. Hung and J. Decety, 'Expertise modulates the perception of pain in others', *Current Biology*, 2007, 17, 1,708–13

22. T. Singer, B. Seymour, J. O'Doherty, H. Kaube, R. J. Dolan and C. D. Frith, 'Empathy for pain involves the affective but not sensory components of pain', *Science*, 2004, 303, 1,157–62

23. M. Botvinick, A. P. Jha, L. M. Bylsma, S. A. Fabian, P. E. Solomon and K. M. Prkachin, 'Viewing facial expressions of pain engages cortical areas involved in the direct experience of pain', *Neuroimage*, 2005, 25, 312–19

24. For more information on synaesthesia and its various forms, visit http://en.wikipedia.org/wiki/Synesthesia (last accessed 21 January 2011)

25. S-J. Blakemore, D. Bristow, G. Bird, C. Frith and J. Ward, 'Somatosensory activations during the observation of touch and a case of vision–touch synaesthesia', *Brain*, 2005, 128, 1,571–83

26. H. Thomson, 'Is this proof that spooky auras are real?', *New Scientist*, 14 November 2010, http://www.newscientist.com/blogs/shortsharpscience/2010/11/auras.html#more (last accessed 21 January 2011)

27. M. V. Saarela, Y. Hlushchuk, A. C. Williams, M. Schürmann, F. Kalso and R. Hari, 'The compassionate brain: humans detect intensity of pain from another's face', *Cerebral Cortex*, 2007, 17(1), 230–37

28. M. J. Magnée, J. J. Stekelenburg, C. Kemner and B. de Gelder, 'Similar facial electromyographic responses to faces, voices, and bodily expressions', *Neuroreport*, 2007, 18(4), 369–72

29. Y. Seung, J-S. Kyong, S-H. Woo, B-T. Lee and K-M. Lee, 'Brain activation during music listening in individuals with or without prior music training', *Neuroscience Research*, 2005, 52(4), 323–9. *See also* M. Bangert, T. Peschel, G. Schlaug, M. Rotte, D. Drescher, H. Hinrichs, H-J. Heinze and E. Altenmüller, 'Shared networks for auditory and motor processing in professional pianists: evidence for fMRI conjunction', *Neuroimage*, 2006, 30, 917–26

30. G. Buccino, L. Riggio, G. Melli, F. Binkofski, V. Gallese and G. Rizzolati, 'Listening to action-related sentences modulates the activity of the motor system: a combined TMS and behavioural study', *Cognitive Brain Research*, 2005, 24(3), 355–63

31. V. Gazzola, L. Aziz-Zadeh and C. Keysers, 'Empathy and the somatotopic auditory mirror system in humans', *Current Biology*, 2006, 16, 1,824–9

32. N. A. Harrison, T. Singer, P. Rotshein, R. J. Dolan and H. D. Critchley, 'Pupillary contagion: central mechanisms engaged in sadness processing', *SCAN*, 2006, 1, 5–17

33. K. E. Demos, W. M. Kelley, S. L. Ryan, F. C. Davis and P. J. Whalen, 'Human amygdala sensitivity to the pupil sizes of others', *Cerebral Cortex*, 2008, 18, 2,729–34

34. It is well known that emotions produce biochemical responses throughout the body. When we 'catch' an emotion from someone, we feel it as our own, so our body chemistry will change just as if it were our own. For general information on body chemistry changes in response to mind and emotions, *see* David R. Hamilton, *It's the Thought that Counts*, Hay House, London, 2006; David R. Hamilton, *How Your Mind Can Heal Your Body*, Hay House, London, 2008; Bruce H. Lipton, *The Biology of Belief*, Hay House, London, 2011; Candace B. Pert, *Molecules of Emotion*, Simon & Schuster, New York, 1997

35. F. Nietzsche, *Human, All Too Human: A Book for Free Spirits*, Cambridge University Press, Cambridge, 1996 edition, p.92

### *CHAPTER 2:* ONE GOOD YAWN DESERVES ANOTHER

1. R. R. Provine, 'Yawning', *American Scientist*, 2005, 93, 532–9

2. R. R. Provine, 'Yawning as a stereotyped action pattern and releasing stimulus', *Ethology*, 1986, 72(2), 109–22

3. A. Paukner and J. R. Anderson, 'Video-induced yawning in stumptail macaques (*Macca arctoides*)', *Biology Letters*, 2006, 2(1), 36–8

4. J. R. Anderson, M. Myowa-Yamakoshi and T. Matsuzawa, 'Contagious yawning in chimpanzees', *Proceedings of the Biological Society*, 2004, 271(6), S468–70

5. M. W. Campbell, J. Devyn Carter, D. Proctor, M. L. Eisenberg and F. B. M. de Waal, 'Computer animations stimulate contagious yawning in chimpanzees', *Proceedings of the Royal Society B*, 2009, 270, 4,255–9

6. R. M. Joly-Mascheroni, A. Senju and A. J. Shepherd, 'Dogs catch human yawns', *Biology Letters*, 2008, 23(4), 446–8

7. S. M. Platek, S. R. Critton, T. E. Myers and G. G. Gallup, 'Contagious yawning: the role of self-awareness and mental state attribution', *Brain Research Cognitive Brain Research*, 2003, 17(2), 223–7

8. S. Kotler, 'A Man's 20 Best Friends', *Observer* magazine, 31 October 2010, 36–41

9. E. Palagi, A. Leone, G. Mancini and P. F. Ferrari, 'Contagious yawning in gelada baboons as a possible expression of empathy', *Proceedings of the National Academy of Sciences*, 2009, 106(46), 19,262–7

10. F. B. Nahab, N. Hattori, Z. S. Saad and M. Hallett, 'Contagious yawning and the frontal lobe: an fMRI study', *Human Brain Mapping*, 2009, 30(5), 1,744–51

11. M. Schürmann, M. D. Hesse, K. E. Stephan, M. Saarela, K. Zilles, R. Hari and G. R. Fink, 'Yearning to yawn: the neural basis of contagious yawning', *Neuroimage*, 2005, 24(4), 1,260–64

12. A. Senju, M. Maeda, Y. Kikuchi, T. Hasegawa, Y. Tojo and H. Osanai, 'Absence of contagious yawning in children with autism spectrum disorder', *Biology Letters*, 2007, 3(6), 706–8

13. M. S. Helt, I. M. Eigsti, P. J. Snyder and D. A. Fein, 'Contagious yawning in autistic and typical development', *Child Development*, 2010, 81(5), 1,620–31

14. For a good review of all of the research on contagious yawning, *see* A. Senju, 'Developmental and comparative perspectives of contagious yawning', *Frontiers of Neurology and Neuroscience*, 2010, 28, 113–19

### *CHAPTER 3:* EMOTIONAL CONTAGION STARTS EARLY

1. M. L. Hoffman, 'Toward a Theory of Empathic Arousal and Development' in M. Lewis and L. A. Rosenblum (eds), *The Development of Affect*, Plenum, New York, 1978

2. T. Field, R. Woodson, D. Cohen, R. Garcia, R. Greenberg and K. Collins, 'Discrimination and imitation of facial expressions by term and preterm neonates', *Infant Behaviour Development*, 1983, 6, 485–90. *See also* T. Field, R. Woodson, D. Cohen and R. Greenberg, 'Discrimination and imitation of facial expressions by neonates', *Science*, 1982, 218(4,568), 179–81

3. N. Reissland, 'Neonatal imitation in the first hour of life: observations in rural Nepal', *Developmental Psychology*, 1988, 24(4), 464–9

4. R. L. Webster, M. H. Steinhardt and M. G. Senter, 'Changes in infants' vocalizations as a function of differential acoustic stimulation', *Developmental Psychology*, 1972, 7, 39–43

5. D. Querleu, X. Renard, F. Versyp, L. Paris-Delrue and G. Crèpin, 'Fetal hearing', *European Journal of Obstetrics and Gynecology*, 1988, 28(3), 191–212

6. Research on when infants start to respond to sounds can be found in E. Hatfield, J. T. Cacioppo and R. L. Rapson, *Emotional Contagion*, Cambridge University Press, Cambridge, 1994

7. http://www.theaustralian.com.au/news/nation/fetus-captured-on-film-smiling-at-just-17-weeks/story-cOfrgCnf 1225006817667 (laot aooooood 21 January 2011)

8. J. P. Lecanuet, C. Granier-Deferre, A. J. DeCasper, R. Maugeais, A. J. Andrieu and M. C. Busnel, 'Perception et discrimination foetales de stimuli langagiers, mises en evidence à partir de la réactivité cardiaque, résultats préliminaires', *Compte Rendus de l'Académie de Sciences, Paris (III)*, 1987, 305, 161–4

9. F. Z. Zimmer, W. P. Fifer, Y-I. Kim, H. R. Rey, C. R. Chao and M. M. Myers, 'Response of the premature fetus to stimulation by speech sounds', *Early Human Development*, 1993, 33(3), 207–15. *See also* L. J. Groome, D. M. Mooney, S. B. Holland, L. A. Smith, J. L. Atterbury and R. A. Dykman, 'Behavioural state affects heart rate response to low-intensity sound in human fetuses', *Early Human Development*, 1999, 54, 39–54

10. J. P. Lecanuet, C. Granier-Deferre, A. Y. Jacquet, I. Capponi and L. Ledru, 'Prenatal discrimination of a male and female voice uttering the same sentence', *Early Development and Parenting*, 1993, 2, 217–28

11. B. S. Kisilevsky, S. M. J. Hains, K. Lee, Z. Xie, H. Huang, H. H. Ye, K. Zhang and Z. Wang, 'Effects of experience on fetal voice recognition', *Psychological Science*, 2003, 14(3), 220–24

12. M. Bozzette, 'Healthy preterm infant responses to taped maternal voices', *Journal of Perinatal and Neonatal Nursing*, 2008, 22(4), 307–16

13. Y. Saito, S. Aoyama, T. Kondo, R. Fukumoto, N. Konishi, K. Nakamura, M. Kobayashi and T. Toshima, 'Frontal cerebral blood flow change associated with infant directed speech', *Archives of Disease in Childhood – Fetal and Neonatal Edition*, 2007, 92, F113–16

14. A. J. DeCasper and W. P. Fifer, 'Of human bonding: newborns prefer their mother's voices', *Science*, 1980, 208(448), 1,174–6

15. C. Valiente, N. Eisenberg, S. A. Shepard, R. A. Fabes, A. J. Cumberland, S. H. Losoya and T. L. Spinrad, *Journal of Applied Developmental Psychology*, 2004, 25(2), 215–35

16. E. M. Cummings, 'Coping with background anger in early childhood', *Child Development*, 1987, 58, 976–84

17. W. M. Troxel and K. A. Mathews, 'What are the costs of marital conflict and dissolution to children's physical health?' *Clinical Child and Family Psychology Review*, 2004, 7(1), 29–57

18. J. M. Gottman and L. F. Katz, 'Effects of marital discord on young children's peer interaction and health', *Developmental Psychology*, 1989, 25(3), 373–81

19. D. A. Dawson, 'Family structure and children's health and wellbeing: data from the 1988 National Health Interview

Survey on child health', *Journal of Marriage and the Family*, 1991, 53, 573–84

20. E. H. Maier and M. E. Lachman, 'Consequences of early parental loss and separation for health and well-being in midlife', *International Journal of Behaviour Development*, 2000, 24(2), 183–9

21. P. R. Amato, 'Children of divorce in the 1990s: an update on the Amato and Keith (1991) meta-analysis', *Journal of Family Psychology*, 2001, 15(3), 355–70

22. http://www.thefullwiki.org/Jonathan_Davis (last accessed 21 January 2011)

23. T. Field, M. Diego and M. Hernandez-Reif, 'Prenatal depression effects on the fetus and newborn: a review', *Infant Behaviour and Development*, 2006, 29(3), 445–55

24. T. Field, M. Diego and M. Hernandez-Reif, 'Infants of depressed mothers are less responsive to faces and voices: a review', *Infant Behaviour and Development*, 2009, 32(3), 239–44

25. M. Hernandez-Reif, T. Field, M. Diego, Y. Vera and J. Pickens, 'Happy faces are habituated more slowly by infants of depressed mothers', *Infant Behaviour and Development*, 2006, 29(1), 131–5

26. T. Field, M. Diego, M. Hernandez-Reif and M. Fernandez, 'Depressed mothers' newborns show less discrimination of other newborns' cry sounds', *Infant Behaviour and Development*, 2007, 30, 431–5

27. N. A. Jones, T. Field and M. Davalos, 'Right frontal EEG asymmetry and lack of empathy in preschool children of depressed mothers', *Child Psychiatry and Human Development*, 2000, 30(3), 189–204

28. B. A. Bettes, 'Maternal depression and motherese: temporal and intonational features', *Child Development*, 1988, 59, 1,089–96

29. G. Downey and J. C. Coyne, 'Children of depressed parents', *Psychological Bulletin* 108, 1990, 50–76

30. http://www.health.com/health/condition-article/ 0,,20214527_1,00.html (last accessed 21 January 2011)

31. http://www.health.com/health/condition-article/ 0,,20214527_1,00.html (last accessed 21 January 2011)

32. N. M. Slough, R. J. McMahon, K. L. Bierman, J. D. Cole, K. A. Dodge, E. M. Foster, M. T. Greenberg, J. E. Lochman and E. E. Pinderhughes, 'Preventing serious conduct problems in school-age youths: the Fast Track Program', *Cognitive and Behavioural Practice*, 2008, 15(1), 3–17

33. Ibid.

34. Ibid.

35. T. Fields, O. Deeds, M. Hernandez-Reif, A. Gauler, S. Sullivan, D. Wilson and G. Nearing, 'Benefits of combining massage therapy with group interpersonal psychotherapy in prenatally depressed women', *Journal of Bodywork and Movement Therapies*, 2009, 13(4), 297–303

36. http://en.wikipedia.org/wiki/Adolescent_psychology (last accessed 21 January 2011)

37. M. Gardner and L. Steinberg, 'Peer influence on risk taking, risk preference, and risky decision making in adolescence and adulthood: an experimental study', *Developmental Psychology*, 2005, 41(4), 625–35

38. M. J. Prinstein, 'Moderators of peer contagion: a longitudinal examination of depression socialization between adolescents and their best friends', *Journal of Clinical Child and Adolescent Psychology*, 2007, 36(2), 159–70

39. W. E. Ellis and L. Zarbatany, 'Peer group status as a moderator of group influence on children's deviant, aggressive and prosocial behaviour', *Child Development*, 2007, 78(4), 1,240–54

40. G. L. Cohen and M. J. Prinstein, 'Peer contagion of aggression and health risk behaviour among adolescent males: an experimental investigation of effects on public conduct and private attitudes', *Child Development*, 2006, 77(4), 967–83

41. L. Steinberg and K. C. Monahan, 'Age differences in resistance to peer pressure', *Developmental Psychology*, 2007, 43(6), 1,531–43, 1,531

42. P. Boxer, N. G. Guerra, L. R. Huesmann and J. Morales, 'Proximal peer-level effects of a small-group selected prevention of aggression in elementary school children: an investigation of the peer contagion hypothesis', *Journal of Abnormal Child Psychology*, 2005, 33(3), 325–38

43. T. J. Berndt, 'Developmental changes in conformity to peers and parents', *Developmental Psychology*, 1979, 15(6), 608–16

44. Steinberg and Monahan, op. cit.

### *CHAPTER 4:* CONTAGION FROM VIDEO GAMES

1. C. A. Anderson, A. Sakamoto, D. A. Gentile, N. Ihori, A. Shibuya, S. Yukawa, M. Naito and K. Kobayashi, 'Longitudinal effects of violent video games on aggression in Japan and

the United States', *Pediatrics*, 2008, 122(5), e1,067–72. *See also* S. Martin and K. Oppenheim, 'Video gaming: general and pathological use', *Trends and Tudes*, 2007, 6(3), 1–7, *and* M. B. Harris and R. Williams, 'Video games and school performance', *Education*, 1985, 105(3), 306–9

2.  United States Department of Health and Human Services, 'Youth violence: a report of the surgeon general', 2001, http://www.surgeongeneral.gov/library/youthviolence/ (last accessed 21 January 2011)

3.  C. A. Anderson, 'An update on the effects of playing violent video games', *Journal of Adolescence*, 2004, 27, 113–22

4.  B. J. Bushman and C. A. Anderson, 'Comfortably numb: desensitizing effects of violent media on helping others', *Psychological Science*, 2009, 20(3), 273–7

5.  Ibid.

6.  http://psychology.wikia.com/wiki/Bystander_intervention (last accessed 21 January 2011)

7.  B. D. Bartholow, B. J. Bushman and M. A. Sestir, 'Chronic violent video game exposure and desensitization to violence: behavioral and event-related brain potential data', *Journal of Experimental Social Psychology*, 2006, 42, 532–9

8.  N. L. Carnagey, C. A. Anderson and B. J. Bushman, 'The effect of video game violence on physiological desensitization to real-life violence', *Journal of Experimental Social Psychology*, 2007, 43, 489–96

9.  C. J. Ferguson, 'The good, the bad, and the ugly: a meta-analysis review of positive and negative effects of violent video games', *Psychiatry Quarterly*, 2007, 78(4), 309–16

10. Anderson *et al*, op. cit.

11. I. Möller and B. Krahé, 'Exposure to violent video games and aggression in German adolescents: a longitudinal analysis', *Aggressive Behaviour*, 2009, 35(1), 75–89

12. C. P. Bartlett and C. Rodeheffer, 'Effects of realism on extended violent and nonviolent video game play on aggressive thoughts, feelings, and physiological arousal', *Aggressive Behaviour*, 2009, 35(3), 213–24

13. H. Polman, B. O. de Castro and M. A. van Aken, 'Experimental study of the differential effects of playing versus watching violent video games on children's aggressive behaviour', *Aggressive Behaviour*, 2008, 34(3), 256–64

14. F. Thomas and O. Johnson, *Disney Animation: The Illusion of Life*, Abbeville Press, New York, 1981

## CHAPTER 5: TRANSMITTING EMOTIONS

1. R. Neumann and F. Strack, '"Mood contagion": the automatic transfer of mood between persons', *Journal of Personality and Social Psychology*, 2000, 79(2), 211–23

2. E. Hatfield, J. T. Cacioppo and R. L. Rapson, *Emotional Contagion*, Cambridge University Press, Cambridge, 1994

3. H. S. Friedman and R. E. Riggio, 'Effect of individual differences in nonverbal expressiveness on transmission of emotion', *Journal of Nonverbal Behaviour*, 1981, 6, 96–101

4. E. S. Sullins, 'Emotional contagion revisited: effects of social comparison and expressive style on mood convergence', *Personality and Social Psychology Bulletin*, 1991, 17, 166–74

5. R. Buck, R. E. Miller and W. F. Caul, 'Sex, personality, and physiological variables in the communication of emotion via facial expression', *Journal of Personality and Social Psychology*, 1974, 30, 587–96

6. H. G. Wallbott, 'Big girls don't frown, big boys don't cry – gender differences of professional actors in communicating emotion via facial expression', *Journal of Nonverbal Behaviour*, 1988, 12, 98–106

7. J. A. Hall, *Nonverbal Sex Differences: Communication Accuracy and Expressive Style*, Johns Hopkins University Press, Baltimore, 1984

8. Ibid.

9. J. M. Haviland and C. Z. Malatesta, 'The Development of Sex Differences in Nonverbal Signals: Fallacies, Facts, and Fantasies' in C. Mayo and N. M. Henley (eds), *Gender and Nonverbal Behaviour*, Springer-Verlag, New York, 183–208

10. Letter from HM Prison, Reading, to Robert Ross, in O. Wilde, *Selected Prose of Oscar Wilde*, Icon Group International, San Diego, 2008, p.112

### *CHAPTER 6:* SOAKING UP EMOTIONS

1. E. Hatfield, J. T. Cacioppo and R. L. Rapson, *Emotional Contagion*, Cambridge University Press, Cambridge, 1994

2. C. K. Hsee, E. Hatfield and C. Chemtob, 'Assessment of the emotional states of others: conscious judgments versus emotional contagion', *Journal of Social and Clinical Psychology*, 1992, 11, 119–28

3. C. G. Jung, *Analytical Psychology: Its Theory and Practice*, Random House, New York, 1968, Lecture 5, 155

4. J. Zaki, N. Bolger and K. Ochsner, 'Unpacking the informational bases of empathic accuracy', *Emotion*, 2009, 9(4), 478–87

5. Hsee, Hatfield and Chemtob, op. cit.

6. R. W. Doherty, L. Orimoto, T. M. Singelis, J. Hebb and E. Hatfield, 'Emotional contagion: gender and occupational differences', *Psychology of Women Quarterly*, 1995, 19, 355–71

7. J. M. Haviland and C. Z. Malatesta, 'The Development of Sex Differences in Nonverbal Signals: Fallacies, Facts, and Fantasies' in C. Mayo and N. M. Henley (eds), *Gender and Nonverbal Behavior*, Springer-Verlag, New York, 1981, 183–208

8. H. R. Markus and S. Kitayama, 'Culture and self: implications for cognition, emotion, and motivation', *Psychological Review*, 1991, 98, 224–53

9. R. B. van Baaren, W. W. Maddux, T. L. Chatrand, C. de Bouter and A. van Knipperberg, 'It takes two to mimic: behavioural consequences of self-construals', *Journal of Personality and Social Psychology*, 2003, 84(5), 1,093–102

10. A. L. Paukert, J. W. Pettit and A. Amacker, 'The role of interdependence and perceived similarity in depressed affect contagion', *Behaviour Therapy*, 2008, 39(3), 277–85

### *CHAPTER 7:* 'IT'S NOT MY STUFF': RESISTING EMOTIONAL CONTAGION

1. As there is little scientific research in the area of resisting emotional contagion, some of the strategies in this section are based on my own personal observations derived from

several years of awareness of emotional contagion and demonstrations in workshops

2. S. W. Lazar, C. E. Kerr, R. H. Wasserman, J. R. Gray, D. N. Greve, M. T. Treadway, M. McGarvey, B. T. Quin, J. A. Dusek, H. T. Benson, S. L. Rauch, C. I. Moore and B. Fischl, 'Meditation experience is associated with increased cortical thickness', *Neuroreport*, 2005, 16(17), 1,893–7

3. A. J. Giannini, D. Tamulonis, M. C. Giannini, R. H. Loiselle and G. Spirtos, 'Defective response to social cues in Mobius syndrome', *Journal of Nervous and Mental Disorders*, 1984, 172(3), 174–5

4. D. A. Havas, A. M. Glenberg, K. A. Gutowski, M. J. Lucarelli and R. J. Davidson, 'Cosmetic use of botulinum toxin-A affects processing of emotional language', *Psychological Science*, 2010, 21(7), 895–900

5. A. Hennenlotter, C. Dresel, F. Castrop, A. O. Ceballos-Baumann, A. N. Wohlschläger and B. Haslinger, 'The link between facial feedback and neural activity within central circuitries of emotion: new insights from botulinum toxin-induced denervation of frown muscles', *Cerebral Cortex*, 2009, 19(3), 537–42

6. M. Alam, K. C. Barrett, R. M. Hodapp and K. A. Arndt, 'Botulinum toxin and the facial feedback hypothesis: can looking better make you feel happier?', *Journal of the American Academy of Dermatology*, 2008, 58(6), 1,061–72

*CHAPTER 8:* CONTAGIOUS DEPRESSION

1. Discussed by Dr Chris, *This Morning*, ITV, 9 November 2010

2. Interview with Martin Seligman in J. Buie, '"Me" decades generate depression: individualism erodes commitment to others', *APA Monitor*, 1988, 19, 18

3. J. C. Coyne, 'Depression and the response of others', *Journal of Abnormal Psychology*, 1976, 85, 186–93

4. M. J. Howes, J. E. Hokanson and D. A. Lowenstein, 'Induction of depressive affect after prolonged exposure to a mildly depressed individual', *Journal of Personality and Social Psychology*, 1985, 49, 1,110–13

5. M. J. Siegel, E. H. Bradley, W. T. Gallo and S. V. Kasl, 'The effect of spousal mental and physical health on husbands' and wives' depressive symptoms, among older adults', *Journal of Aging and Health*, 2004, 16, 398–425

6. P. Butterworth and B. Rodgers, 'Concordance in the mental health of spouses: analysis of a large national household panel survey', *Psychological Medicine*, 2006, 36(5), 685–97

7. D. Meyler, J. P. Stimpson and M. K. Peek, 'Health concordance within couples: a systematic review', *Social Sciences in Medicine*, 2007, 64, 2,297–310

8. C. D. Kouros and E. M. Cummings, 'Longitudinal associations between husbands' and wives' depressive symptoms', *Journal of Marriage and Family*, 2010, 72, 135–47

9. J. N. Rosenquist, J. H. Fowler and N. A Christakis, 'Social network determinants of depression', *Molecular Psychiatry*, 2010, 1–9

10. For general information on the Framingham Heart Study, visit http://www.framinghamheartstudy.org (last accessed 21 January 2011)

11. Rosenquist, Fowler and Christakis, op. cit.

12. Depression was measured using the Centre for Epidemiological Studies Depression Scale, where participants were asked how often they had experienced a specific feeling associated with depression over the past week. They could answer 0–1 days (0 points), 1–2 days (1 point), 3–4 days (2 points), or 5–7 days (3 points). The total score after 20 questions allowed people to be labelled as depressed or non-depressed. A score of 16 or more was determined to indicate depression

13. Rosenquist, Fowler and Christakis, op. cit.

14. Martin Luther King Jr, during his Nobel Lecture at the University of Oslo on 11 December 1964

15. D. Mapes, 'Loneliness can be contagious, new study finds'. Interview with John Cacioppo, http://www.msnbc.msn.com/id/34209727/ns/health-behavior/ (last accessed 24 January 2011)

16. J. T. Cacioppo, J. H. Fowler, and N. H. Christakis, 'Alone in the crowd: the structure and spread of loneliness in a large social network', *Journal of Personality and Social Psychology*, 2009, 97(6), 977–91

17. Rosenquist, Fowler and Christakis, op. cit., 9

## *CHAPTER 9:* FROM NON-CONTAGIOUS TO CONTAGIOUS

1. http://www.who.int/mediacentre/factsheets/fs311/en/index.html (last accessed 24 January 2011)

2. http://www.who.int/dietphysicalactivity/childhood/en/ (last accessed 24 January 2011)

3. N. A. Christakis and J. H. Fowler, 'The spread of obesity in a large social network over 32 years', *The New England Journal of Medicine*, 2007, 357(4), 370–79

4. J. Lehrer, 'The buddy system: how medical data revealed the secret to health and happiness', *Wired* magazine, 9 December 2009; http://www.wired.com/medtech/health/magazine/17-10/ff_christakis (last accessed 24 January 2011)

5. L. C. Macken, B. Yates and S. Blancher, 'Concordance of risk factors in female spouses of male patients with coronary heart disease', *Journal of Cardiopulmonary Rehabilitation*, 2000, 20(6), 361–8

6. M. V. Konnov, L. M. Dobordzhginidze, A. D. Deev and N. A. Gratsianskii, 'Spousal concordance for factors related to metabolic syndrome in families of patients with premature coronary heart disease', *Kardiologiia*, 2010, 50(2), 4–8

7. A. A. Gorin, R. R. Wing, J. L. Fava, J. M. Jakacic, R. Jeffrey, D. S. West, K. Brelje and V. G. Dilillo, 'Weight loss treatment influences untreated spouses and the home environment: evidence of a ripple effect', *International Journal of Obesity*, 2008, 32(11), 1,678–84

8. For a good review of the scientific literature, *see* T. W. Smith, K. Glazer, J. M. Ruiz and L. C. Gallo, 'Hostility, anger, aggressiveness, and coronary heart disease: an interpersonal perspective on personality, emotion, and health', *Journal of Personality*, 2004, 72(6), 1,217–70

9. http://en.wikiquote.org/wiki/Talk:Tom_Stoppard (Last accessed 24 January 2011)

10. *See* the 'Roseto effect' in David R. Hamilton, *Why Kindness Is Good for You*, Hay House, London, 2010

11. J. Holt-Lunstad, T. B. Smith and J. B. Layton, 'Social relationships and mortality risk: a meta-analytic review', *PLoS Medicine*, 2010, 7(7), e1,000,316, 1–20

12. In R. A. Spitz, 'Hospitalism: an inquiry into the genesis of psychiatric conditions in early childhood', *Psychoanalytic Study of the Child*, 1945, 1, 53–74

13. J. Bowlby, 'Maternal Care and Mental Health: A Report Prepared on Behalf of the World Health Organization as a Contribution to the United Nations Programme for the Welfare of Homeless Children', World Health Organization, Geneva, 1951, p.179

14. http://www.unicef.bg/public/images/tinybrowser/upload/ PPT per cent20BEIP%20Group%20for%20website.pdf (last accessed 24 January 2011)

15. Ibid.

16. Hamilton, op. cit.

17. http://www.nytimes.com/2010/04/18/magazine/ 18marriage-t.html?_r=1 (last accessed 24 January 2011)

18. For information on oxytocin, *see* Hamilton, op. cit.

19. A. A. Marsh, H. H. Yu, D. S. Pine and R. J. R. Blair, 'Oxytocin improves specific recognition of positive facial expressions', *Psychopharmacology*, 2010, 209(3), 225–32

20. A. J. Guastella, P. B. Mitchell and M. R. Dadds, 'Oxytocin increases gaze to the eye region of human faces', *Biological Psychiatry*, 2008, 63(1), 3–5

21. G. Domes, M. Heinrichs, A. Michel, C. Bergen and S. C. Herpetz, 'Oxytocin improves "mind reading" in humans', *Biological Psychiatry*, 2007, 61(6), 731–3

22. N. A. Harrison, T. Singer, P. Rotshtein, R. J. Dolan and H. D. Critchley, 'Pupillary contagion: central mechanisms engaged in sadness processing', *SCAN*, 2006, 1, 5–17

23. For details of the studies showing the cardioprotective effects of oxytocin, *see* David R. Hamilton, *Why Kindness Is Good for You*, Hay House, London, 2010

24. C. A. Latkin, 'Outreach in natural settings: the use of peer leaders for HIV prevention among injecting drug users' networks', *Public Health Reports*, 1998, 113(1), 151–9

25. A. Neaigus, 'The network approach and interventions to prevent HIV among injection drug users', *Public Health Reports*, 1998, 113(1), 140–50

26. http://www.biographyonline.net/people/diana/charity_work.html (last accessed 24 January 2011)

27. S. Greenfield, S. H. Kaplan, J. E. Ware Jr, E. M. Yano and H. J. Frank, 'Patients' participation in medical care: effects on blood sugar control and quality of life in diabetes', *Journal of General Internal Medicine*, 1988, 3(5), 448–57

28. N. Ambady, J. Koo, R. Rosenthal and C. H. Winograd, 'Physical therapists' nonverbal communication predicts geriatric patients' health outcomes', *Psychology and Aging*, 2002, 17(3), 443–52

29. K. B. Zolnierek and M. R. Dimatteo, 'Physician communication and patient adherence to treatment: a meta-analysis', *Medical Care*, 2009, 47(8), 826–34

### *CHAPTER 10:* CONTAGIOUS FEAR

1. A. Olsson, K. I. Nearing and E. A. Phelps, 'Learning fears by observing others: the neural systems of social fear transmission', *Scan*, 2007, 2, 3–11

2. B. de Gelder, J. Snyder, D. Greve, G. Gerard and N. Hadjikhani, 'Fear fosters flight: a mechanism for fear contagion when perceiving emotion expressed by a whole body', *Proceedings of the National Academy of Sciences*, 2004, 101(47), 16,701–6

3. N. Tinbergen, 'On aims and methods of ethology', *Zeitschrift für Tierpsychologie*, 1963, 20, 410–33

4. S. Mineka, M. Davidson, M. Cook and R. Keir, 'Observational conditioning of fear in Rhesus monkeys', *Journal of Abnormal Psychology*, 1984, 93(4), 355–72

5. M. Cook, S. Mineka, B. Wolkenstein and K. Laitsch, 'Observational conditioning of snake fear in unrelated Rhesus monkeys', *Journal of Abnormal Psychology*, 1985, 94(4), 591–610

6. A. Olsson, K. I. Nearing and E. A. Phelps, 'Learning fears by observing others: the neural systems of social fear transmission', *Scan*, 2007, 2, 3–11, and references within

7. Ibid.

8. T. F. Jones, 'Mass psychogenic illness: role of the individual physician', *American Family Physician*, December 15, 2000; http://www.aafp.org/afp/20001215/2649.html (last accessed 21 January 2011)

9. For general information on mass psychogenic illness, visit http://en.wikipedia.org/wiki/Mass_Psychogenic_Illness (last accessed 21 January 2011)

10. A. Page, C. Keshishian, G. Leonardi, V. Murray, G. J. Rubin and S. Wessely, 'Frequency and predictors of mass psychogenic illness', *Epidemiology*, 2010, 21(5), 744–7

11. R. E. Bartholomew and S. Wessely, 'Protean nature of mass sociogenic illness: from possessed nuns to chemical and biological terrorism', *British Journal of Psychiatry*, 2002, 180, 300–306

12. J. Viegas, '"Dancing plague" and other odd afflictions explained', *Discovery News*, 1 August 2008

13. J. Waller, 'In the spin: the mysterious dancing epidemic of 1518', *Endeavor*, 2008, 32(3), 117–21

14. Jones, op. cit.

15. E. G. Karam and L. H. Khattar, 'Mass psychogenic illness (epidemic sociogenic attacks) in a village in Lebanon', *Lebanese Medical Journal*, 2007, 55(2), 112–15

16. Jones, op. cit.

17. David R. Hamilton, *How Your Mind Can Heal Your Body*, Hay House, London, 2008

18. Y. T. Lee and S. J. Tsai, 'The mirror neuron system may play a role in the pathogenesis of mass hysteria', *Medical Hypotheses*, 2010, 74(2), 244–5

19. R. Goodwin, S. Haque, F. Neto and L. B. Meyers, 'Initial psychological responses to influenza A, H1N1 ("swine flu")', *BMC Infectious Diseases*, 2009, 9, 166–71

20. S. Mineka and M. Cook, 'Immunization against the observational conditioning of snake fear in Rhesus monkeys', *Journal of Abnormal Psychology*, 1986, 95(4), 307–18

21. Nelson Mandela, *Long Walk to Freedom*, Abacus, London, 1995, p.756

### *CHAPTER 11:* THE POWER OF POSITIVE PEOPLE

1. S. G. Barsade, 'The ripple effect: emotional contagion and its influence on group behaviour', *Administrative Science Quarterly*, 2002, 47(4), 644–75

2. N. Eisenkraft and H. A. Elfenbein, 'The way you make me feel: evidence for individual differences in affective presence', *Psychological Science*, 2010, 21(4), 505–10

3. A. M. Isen, K. A. Daubman and G. P. Nowicki, 'Positive affect facilitates creative problem solving', *Journal of Personality and Social Psychology*, 1987, 52(6), 1,122–31

4. R. Ilies and T. A Judge, 'Goal regulation across time: the effects of feedback and affect', *Journal of Applied Psychology*, 2005, 90(3), 453–67

5. K. D. Bramesfield and K. Gasper, 'Happily putting the pieces together: a test of two explanations for the effects of mood on group-level information processing', *British Journal of Social Psychology*, 2008, 47(Pt 2), 285–309

6. A. M. Isen and R. A. Baron, 'Positive Affect as a Factor in Organizational Behaviour' in *Research in Organizational Behaviour*, B. M. Staw and L. L. Cummings (eds), JAI Press, Greenwich, CT, 1991, 1–53, 13

7. S. Djamasbi, 'Does positive affect influence the effective usage of a Decision Support System?' *Decisions Support Systems*, 2007, 43(4), 1,707–17

8. C. A. Estrada, A. M. Isen and M. J. Young, 'Positive affect facilitates integration of information and decreases anchoring in reasoning among physicians', *Organizational Behaviour and Human Decision Processes*, 1997, 72(1), 117–35

9. D. Piquette, S. Reeves and V. R. LeBlanc, 'Stressful intensive care unit medical crises: how individual responses impact on team performance', *Critical Care Medicine*, 2009, 37(4), 1,251–5

10. R. G. Netemeyer, J. G. Maxham and D. R. Lichenstein, 'Store manager performance and satisfaction: effects on store employee performance and satisfaction, store customer satisfaction, and store customer spending growth', *Journal of Applied Psychology*, 2010, 95(3), 530–45

11. F. Rhul, 'Group emotion and leadership', *Psychiatry: Journal for the Study of Interpersonal Processes*, 1942, 5, 573–96

12. T. Sy, S. Côté and R. Saavedra, 'The contagious leader: impact of the leader's mood on the mood of group members, group affective tone, and group processes', *Journal of Applied Psychology*, 2005, 90(2), 295–305

13. J. M. George, 'Leader positive mood and group performance: the case of customer service', *Journal of Applied Social Psychology*, 1995, 25(9), 778–94

14. Corporate Executive Board, 'Linking Employee Satisfaction with Productivity, Performance, and Customer Satisfaction', Corporate Leadership Council paper, July 2003, www.corporateleadershipcouncil.com

15. P. Totterdell, S. Kellett, K. Teuchmann and R. B. Briner, 'Evidence of mood linkage in work groups', *Journal of Personality and Social Psychology*, 1998, 74(6), 1,504–15

16. P. Totterdell, 'Catching moods and hitting runs: mood linkage and subjective performance in professional sports teams', *Journal of Applied Psychology*, 2000, 85(6), 848–59

17. T. Moll, G. Jordet and G. J. Pepping, 'Emotional contagion in soccer penalty shootouts: celebration of individual success is associated with ultimate team success', *Journal of Sports Science*, 2010, 28(9), 983–92

18. K. S. Dallimore, B. A. Sparks and K. Butcher, 'The influence of angry customer service outbursts on service providers' facial displays and affective states', *Journal of Service Research*, 2007, 10(1), 78–92

19. A. A. Grandey, D. N. Dickter and H-P. Sin, 'The customer is *not* always right: customer aggression and emotion regulation of service employees', *Journal of Organizational Behaviour*, 2004, 25, 1–22

20. P. D. Cherulnik, K. A. Donley, T. S. R. Wiewel and S. R. Miller, 'Charisma is contagious: the effect of leaders' charisma on observers' affect', *Journal of Applied Social Psychology*, 2001, 31(10), 2,149–59

21. J. E. Bono and R. Ilies, 'Charisma, positive emotions and mood contagion', *The Leadership Quarterly*, 2006, 17, 317–34

22. J. K. Burgoon, 'Nonverbal Signals' in M. L. Knapp and G. R. Miller (eds), *Handbook of Interpersonal Communication*, Sage Publications, Beverly Hills, 1985, 344–90

23. ICON Group, *Belittling: Webster's Quotations, Facts, and Phrases*, ICON Group International, Inc., San Diego, 2008, p.1

### *CHAPTER 12:* THERE'S POWER IN YOUR FACE

1. M. W. Morris, 'Rapport in conflict resolution: accounting for how face-to-face contact fosters mutual cooperation

in mixed motive conflicts', *Journal of Experimental Social Psychology*, 2000, 36, 26–50

2. E. Hatfield and E. Sprecher, *Mirror, Mirror: The Importance of Looks in Everyday Life*, SUNY Press, Albany, NY, 1986

## *CHAPTER 13:* YOU CAN'T RESIST A SMILE

1. E. Zhivotovskaya, 'Smile and others smile with you: health benefits, emotional contagion, and mimicry', *Positive News Daily*, 27 September 2008; http://positivepsychologynews. com/news/emiliya zhivotovokaya/200809271036 (last accessed 21 January 2011)

2. U. Dimberg, M. Thunberg and S. Grunedal, 'Facial reactions to emotional stimuli: automatically controlled emotional responses', *Cognition and Emotion*, 2002, 16(4), 449–71

3. P. Ekman, R. J. Davidson and W. V. Friesen, 'The Duchenne smile: emotional expression and brain physiology II', *Journal of Personality and Social Psychology*, 1990, 58(2), 342–53

4. L-A. Harker and D. Keltner, 'Expressions of positive emotion in women's college yearbook pictures and their relationship to personality and life outcomes across adulthood', *Journal of Personality and Social Psychology*, 2001, 80(1), 112–24

5. http://en.wikipedia.org/wiki/Facial_feedback_hypothesis (last accessed 21 January 2011)

6. C. Darwin, *The Expression of Emotions in Man and Animals*, John Murray, London, 1872

7. P. Ekman, 'An argument for basic emotions', *Cognition and Emotion*, 1992, 6(3/4), 169–200

8.  A. R. Damasio, T. J. Grabowski, A. Bechara, H. Damasio, L. L. B. Ponto, J. Parvizi and R. D. Hichwa, 'Subcortical and cortical brain activity during the feeling of self-generated emotions', *Nature Neuroscience*, 2000, 3(10), 1,049–56

9.  W. James, *The Principles of Psychology*, 1890, pp.449, 450

10. http://en.wikipedia.org/wiki/James–Lange_theory (last accessed 24 January 2011)

11. C. L. Kleinke, T. R. Peterson and T. R. Rutledge, 'Effects of self-generated facial expressions on mood', *Journal of Personality and Social Psychology*, 1998, 74(1), 272–9

12. A. Freitas-Magalhães and E. Castro, 'Facial Expression: The Effect of the Smile in the Treatment of Depression: Empirical Study with Portuguese Subjects' in A. Freitas-Magalhães (ed.), *Emotional Expression: The Brain and the Face*, University Fernando Pessoa Press, Porto, 2009, 127–40

13. http://www.atencionsanmiguel.org/archives/colu_well_2006_may_05_eng.html (last accessed 24 January 2011)

14. For Cliff Huhn's thoughts on smiling, visit: http://www.natural-humor-medicine.com/depression.html (last accessed 24 January 2011)

15. http://www.finestquotes.com/quote-id-12162.htm (last accessed 21 January 2011)

16. J. E. Warren, D. A. Sauter, F. Eisner, J. Wiland, M. Alexander Dresner, R. J. S. Wise, S. Rosen and S. K. Scott, 'Positive emotions preferentially engage and auditory-motor "mirror" system', *Journal of Neuroscience*, 2006, 26(50), 13,067–75

17. V. Hugo, *Hugo's Works: Les Miserables (Cosette)*, Wildside Press, Rockville, Maryland, 2007, p.299

18. A. Jamieson, 'One Smile Can Make You Feel a Million Dollars', *The Scotsman*, 4 March 2005; http://thescotsman. scotsman.com/health/One-smile-can-make-you.2607641. jp (last accessed 24 January 2011)

19 *The Human Face*, BBC documentary broadcast in four parts, 7–25 March 2001. The study was featured in Part 4

### CHAPTER 14: CAN YOU CATCH HAPPINESS?
1. J. H. Fowler and N. A. Christakis, 'Dynamic spread of happiness in a large social network: longitudinal analysis over 20 years in the Framingham Heart Study', *British Medical Journal*, 2008, 337, a2,338, 1–9

2. Ibid.

3. Khalil Gibran, *The Prophet*, Pan Books, London, 1991 edition, p.80

4. Fowler and Christakis, op. cit.

5. http://www.dailymail.co.uk/health/article-1278560/Want-live-100-Then-nice-friends-family.html (last accessed 21 January 2011)

6. Ibid.

7. Albert Schweitzer, *Philosophy of Civilization*, 1923, Ch.26

### CHAPTER 15: IS KINDNESS CONTAGIOUS?
1. Cited in Dacher Keltner, *Born to Be Good: The Science of a Meaningful Life*, Norton, New York, 2009

2. Ibid.

3. D. C. McClelland and C. Kirshnit, 'The effect of motivational arousal through films on salivary immunoglobulin A', *Psychology and Health*, 1988, 2(1), 31–52

4. J. H. Fowler and N. A. Christakis, 'Cooperative behavior cascades in human social networks', *Proceedings of the National Academy of Sciences*, 2010, 107, 5,334–8

5. R. B. van Baaren, R. W. Holland, K. Kawakami and A. van Knippenberg, 'Mimicry and prosocial behaviour', *Psychological Science*, 2003, 15, 71–4

6. Ibid.

7. Ibid.

8. H. Over and M. Carpenter, 'Eighteen-month-old infants show increased helping following priming with affiliation', *Psychological Science*, 2009, 20(10), 1,189–93

9. R. van Baaren, L. Janssen, T. L. Chatrand and A. Dijksterhuis, 'Where is the love? The social aspects of mimicry', *Philosophical Transactions of the Royal Society B*, 2009, 364(1,528), 2,381–9

10. C. Ashton-James, R. B. van Baaren, T. L. Chatrand, J. Decety and J. Karremans, 'Mimicry and me: the impact of mimicry on self-construal', *Social Cognition*, 2007, 25, 518–35

## *CHAPTER 16:* SINGLE ACTS CAN MAKE A BIG DIFFERENCE

1. For an example of a donor chain, *see* http://www.youtube.com/watch?v=p3xNrlp2y30 (last viewed 24 January 2011)

2. M. A. Rees, J. E. Kopke, R. P. Pelletier, D. L. Segev, M. E. Rutter, A. J. Fabrega, J. Rogers, O. G. Pankewycz, J. Hiller,

A. E. Roth, T. Sandholm, M. U. Ünver and R. A. Montgomery, 'A nonsimultaneous, extended, altruistic-donor chain', *New England Journal of Medicine*, 2009, 360, 1,096–101

3. http://www.anthonyrobbinsfoundation.org/join_the_basket_brigade/ (last accessed 21 January 2011)

4. For a history of the NAACP, visit http://en.wikipedia.org/wiki/National_Association_for_the_Advancement_of_Colored_People

5. Speech made on the evening of 5 December 1955 at Holt Street Baptist Church, Montgomery. Visit: http://www.mlkonline.net/mia.html (last accessed on 21 January 2011)

6. Speech made on 28 August 1963 at an address on a march on Washington, DC. Visit: http://www.mlkonline.net/dream.html (last accessed 21 January 2011)

7. For history of the Niagara Movement, visit http://en.wikipedia.org/wiki/Niagara_Movement (last accessed 21 January 2011)

8. Billy Graham, 'A Time for Moral Courage', *Reader's Digest*, July 1964

9. Quoted in J. Templeton, *Worldwide Laws of Life: 200 Eternal Spiritual Principles*, Templeton Foundation Press, 1998, p.448

# INDEX

negative behaviour
  in adolescents 46–47
  transmitting 65, 66–67
negative emotions
  customer service staff and
    147–150
  importance for forming bonds
    73–74
  resisting 85–90
negative environments
  breeding negative emotions
    89–90
  effect of on babies and
    children 32, 37–42
  methods of combating 87–90
negative memories 90
negotiation, effective 156 (see
  also conflict resolution)
neighbours, contagiousness and
  183, 187
network interventions 122–124
neuro-linguistic programming
  (NLP) 9
neurons, mirror see mirror
  neurons
newborn babies see babies
Niagara Movement 206
NLP (neuro-linguistic
  programming) 9
nocebo effect 129–130, 132–
  133
non-verbal communication 124–
  126, 156–160 (see also body
  language; eye contact; facial
  expressions)
nursing homes, social
  connections in 189

obesity xi, 9, 107–113, 115, 116
orbicularis oculi muscle 92, 121,
  169
organ donor chains 201–202

oxytocin 119–122

pain 13–15, 17–18, 53–55, 56,
  87, 88–89
parental depression 37–42, 115
parental influence
  adolescents and 48–49
  compared to impact of
    television 52
  over their babies and foetuses
    29–34
parenting skills programmes
  43–44
Parks, Rosa 205–207
paternal depression 40
patient outcomes, improving
  124–126
patient relationships 74–75, 89,
  124–126
Pavlov, Ivan 18
peacemaking 155–160
peer pressure 45–49, 52
performance, job see job
  performance and satisfaction
phone calls 96, 157, 180
physical distance, friendships and
  183–184
physical exercise 3–5, 111–112
physiology 87–88, 155–156,
  173–175
placebo effect 130, 132–133
plague 130–134
positive affective tone 142–144
positive behaviour
  bringing out 160–164
  transmitting 66–68
positive emotions 150–152,
  153–154
positive home environment, effect
  on children 196–197
positivity, the power of 135–154,
  160–164

# NOTES

# NOTES

## HAY HOUSE TITLES OF RELATED INTEREST

*The Biology of Belief*,
by Bruce Lipton

*Change Your Thoughts, Change Your Life*,
by Wayne W. Dyer PhD

*How Your Mind Can Heal Your Body*,
by David R. Hamilton PhD

*It's the Thought That Counts*,
by David R. Hamilton PhD

*Rock, Paper, Scissors*,
by Len Fisher

*Virus of the Mind*,
by Richard Brodie

*Why Kindness Is Good for You*,
by David R. Hamilton PhD

# JOIN THE HAY HOUSE FAMILY

As the leading self-help, mind, body and spirit publisher in the UK, we'd like to welcome you to our family so that you can enjoy all the benefits our website has to offer.

 **EXTRACTS** from a selection of your favourite author titles

 **COMPETITIONS, PRIZES & SPECIAL OFFERS** Win extracts, money off, downloads and so much more

 **LISTEN** to a range of radio interviews and our latest audio publications

 **CELEBRATE YOUR BIRTHDAY** An inspiring gift will be sent your way

 **LATEST NEWS** Keep up with the latest news from and about our authors

 **ATTEND OUR AUTHOR EVENTS** Be the first to hear about our author events

 **iPHONE APPS** Download your favourite app for your iPhone

 **HAY HOUSE INFORMATION** Ask us anything, all enquiries answered

join us online at **www.hayhouse.co.uk**

 292B Kensal Road, London W10 5BE
T: 020 8962 1230 E: info@hayhouse.co.uk

# ABOUT THE AUTHOR

 **David R. Hamilton** gained a first-class honours degree in chemistry, specializing in biological and medical chemistry, and a PhD in organic chemistry, before going on to be a scientist in the pharmaceutical industry in 1995. Over the next four years, David worked for one of the world's largest pharmaceutical companies, and also served as an athletics coach and team manager for one of the UK's top athletics clubs. He left both roles in 1999. In 2000 he co-founded Spirit Aid Foundation, an international relief charity helping children whose lives have been affected by war and poverty. In 2002, as a director of Spirit Aid, he helped produce a nine-day, 24-event festival of peace in Glasgow. He served as a director of Spirit Aid until the end of 2002. From 2004 until 2005, he taught chemistry and ecology at James Watt College of Further and Higher Education and tutored chemistry at the University of Glasgow.

In 2005, he self-published his first book, *It's the Thought That Counts*, which was published by Hay House in 2006. David is now the author of five books, all published by Hay House. He has been featured on TV and radio and been the subject of numerous national newspaper articles. He spends most of his time writing, giving talks and leading workshops. David also writes a regular blog for The Huffington Post

www.drdavidhamilton.com